Principals Avoiding Lawsuits

Hodges

Principals Avoiding Lawsuits

How Teachers Can Be Partners in Practicing Preventive Law

David Schimmel, Suzanne Eckes,
and
Matthew Militello

ROWMAN & LITTLEFIELD
Lanham • Boulder • New York • London

Published by Rowman & Littlefield
A wholly owned subsidiary of The Rowman & Littlefield Publishing Group, Inc.
4501 Forbes Boulevard, Suite 200, Lanham, Maryland 20706
www.rowman.com

Unit A, Whitacre Mews, 26-34 Stannary Street, London SE11 4AB

British Library Cataloguing in Publication Information Available

Library of Congress Cataloging-in-Publication Data

Names: Schimmel, David, author. | Eckes, Suzanne, author. |
   Militello, Matthew, author.
Title: Principals avoiding lawsuits: how teachers can be partners in
   practicing preventive law / David Schimmel, Suzanne Eckes, and
   Matthew Militello.
Other titles: Principals teaching the law
Description: Lanham : Rowman & Littlefield, 2017. | Includes index.
Identifiers: LCCN 2016049785 (print) | LCCN 2016059845 (ebook) |
   ISBN 9781475831184 (cloth : alk. paper) | ISBN 9781475831191 (pbk. : alk. paper) |
   ISBN 9781475831207 (electronic)
Subjects: LCSH: School principals—Legal status, laws, etc.—United States. |
   Educational law and legislation—United States. | Tort liability of school
   districts—United States. | Preventive law—United States.
Classification: LCC KF4133 .S349 2017 (print) | LCC KF4133 (ebook) |
   DDC 344.73/075—dc23
LC record available at https://lccn.loc.gov/2016049785

Printed in the United States of America

Contents

Introduction and Overview

The goal of this book is to avoid lawsuits by enabling principals to become better informed and effective teachers of preventive law. Although teaching law is not in their job description, principals *are* the chief law teachers in their schools. This is because principals frequently give informal legal advice—in staff meetings, in their office, in hallway conversations, and in the way they develop, interpret, and enforce school rules. While this legal advice is often appropriate, there are many times when it is confusing, misleading, and incomplete.

This advice (or lack of advice) often leads to two types of mistakes by teachers: failing to take appropriate action when they should and unintentionally violating students' rights when they should not. In either case, teachers inadvertently act (or don't act) on wrong information—putting themselves and their schools in jeopardy. Our purpose is to empower educators to act in the best interest of themselves, their schools, and their students *by knowing the law*!

THE RESULTS OF LEGAL ILLITERACY

Because the vast majority of teachers have not taken a course in school law in their pre- or in-service programs, they are not aware that they function as agents of the government and are therefore restrained by the Bill of Rights as it applies to the public schools. As a result, teachers may unintentionally violate students' constitutional rights when they require them to stand for the Pledge of Allegiance, search their backpacks for possible contraband without reasonable suspicion, or punish them for critical Internet communications that might offend a teacher or administrator.

Teachers' lack of awareness of students' rights can cause friction, frustration, and litigation. This was illustrated by a high school principal who explained, "It's the legal misunderstandings with students, parents and teachers that take up much of my time." For example, she told about one of her teachers who sent a student to her office to be suspended for refusing her order to take off an "offensive" T-shirt. It said the president was the "Founder of ISIS." Unlike the teacher, the principal knew that the student had a First Amendment right to wear the shirt because it caused no disruption, and she refused to suspend him. As a result, the teacher felt embarrassed and unsupported by her principal. On the other hand, if the principal had "supported" her teacher and suspended the student, this probably would have led to a conflict with the parents and a possible lawsuit that the school would have lost.

Additionally, the failure of teachers to act when they should is often the result of oversimplified administrative warnings. According to a national survey (Schimmel & Militello, 2007), the most frequent legal advice principals give to teachers is "Don't touch students." Because of this and other "thou shalt nots," many teachers view law as a source of fear and anxiety. Thus an elementary teacher reported that he does not break up fights among his first graders because he is afraid that if he does, and if a student is injured, he could be found liable for the injury, disciplined by his principal, or both. This widespread belief among teachers that *any* touching of students involves inherent legal dangers persists despite the fact that it is always legal and appropriate for teachers to use reasonable force to protect their students or themselves.

In sum, legally illiterate teachers may fail to take appropriate action—ignoring misbehavior, permitting disruptions, or rescinding reasonable discipline because of meritless threats by parents or students. In addition, when teachers are unaware of how the Bill of Rights protects public school students, they may unintentionally violate students' rights regarding free speech, due process, or search and seizure. These negative consequences of legal illiteracy are compounded by the fact that teachers get much of their legal advice from colleagues who are similarly uninformed or misinformed.

BENEFITS OF LEGAL LITERACY

If principals teach the basic principles of school law as a regular part of their teachers' professional development program, there can be a number of positive results. For example, schools would not be found liable for student injuries when teachers understand and carry out their duty of care to supervise their students. In addition, when teachers understand the laws that govern discipline and the reasonable use of force, they will not be afraid to break up a fight among first graders because of unfounded fears that they could be held personally liable if a student is injured. Nor will teachers fear a lawsuit if they physically restrain an emotionally disabled student who is rushing out of the school toward a dangerous street.

Furthermore, if public school teachers understand that they are agents of the government and are therefore restrained by the Constitution, they are likely to pause and consult with their principal before they search a student or her cell phone, or demand that a student take off a controversial political T-shirt because they fear it might offend someone.

When principals become effective law teachers, their staffs will get their information about school law from a reliable source—not from the rumors, fears, and myths of the teachers' lounge. As practitioners of preventive law, teachers will know when to consult with informed administrators. By having a legally literate staff, principals will benefit because of fewer legal mistakes and misunderstandings by teachers. This should reduce the unnecessary time and energy principals now have to devote to teachers' legal confusions and to preventable parental complaints, threats, and possible litigation—freeing principals to focus on quality teaching and learning. Thus there are multiple benefits to having legally literate staff. We have written this book to make this happen.

With this information, teachers will no longer see themselves as potential victims of the law nor be confused about their legal rights and responsibilities. Instead, they will be empowered with legal knowledge enabling them, in a constructive sense, to "take the law into their own hands." As a result, they will be able, in partnership with their principal, to prevent lawsuits by upholding the law with confidence and by protecting their students, their school, and themselves.

WHO CAN USE THIS BOOK

We do not presume the user of this book has an advanced knowledge of school law. Rather, we presume the users wants to provide themselves and their colleagues with a basic knowledge of school law so that the law does not hamper their ability to be an effective educator. Therefore, we see a number of users for this book:

- *Current principals and assistant-principals* who are looking for materials and methods to be effective teachers of preventive law and who are seeking a reference and update
- *Professional Development Coordinators* can use this book to plan a legal orientation for new teachers and for in-service days throughout the school year
- *Aspiring principals* seeking knowledge they will need to lead the schools of tomorrow
- *Current teachers* seeking answers to common concerns about what to do when confronted with legal situations
- *Superintendents* working directly and collaboratively with their principals
- *Instructors in teacher- and principal-preparation programs* seeking a practical guide to preventative school law
- *District administrators* seeking content for new-teacher orientation and extended-day and summer professional-development opportunities
- *School board members* who need to be knowledgeable of school-law issues (e.g., in Massachusetts, board members are required by law to attend an orientation that includes school law)
- *Other school personnel (e.g., guidance counselors, school nurses, paraprofessionals, bus drivers, school security, and resource officers)* who also confront legal issues in schools

HOW WE ORGANIZED THE BOOK

We selected ten lesson plans to present in this book. While other topic areas could have certainly been included, we selected these ten lessons on the basis of our research that has highlighted the most frequent or common questions schoolteachers and principals ask about school law. We also used topics that are timely and relevant. That is, we often included cases that have been highly publicized by the media and the courts. The table below summarizes the ten law topics we selected.

Lesson Plan	Description
1. Liability for Student Injuries	When can teachers be held liable for student injuries that occur in their classrooms or when they are on duty in the hallways or playgrounds? Can teachers be held liable if a student is injured when they break up a fight or drive a student in their car? Can they restrain a disruptive student? Are there state or federal laws that protect teachers against being held liable? Does insurance or parental waivers protect them? Does a teacher's duty of care vary with the age of the student?
2. Student Freedom of Expression	What is the scope and limits of student freedom of expression in the public schools? Can teachers prohibit messages on student T-shirts that are controversial, offensive, or vulgar? Can schools prohibit students from distributing unapproved newspapers or flyers on campus? Can students be punished for messages on their websites that insult teachers, criticize school policies, or might cause disruption?
3. Special Education	When is a student entitled to special rights under IDEA (Individuals with Disabilities Education Act) and under Section 504 of the Rehabilitation Act of 1973? What constitutes a free appropriate public education under IDEA? What is required in an IEP (individualized education program)? Do all teachers have responsibilities to implement IEPs? What is meant by "the least restrictive environment" and "related services"? What "reasonable accommodations" must be made under Section 504?
4. Student Due Process and Search and Seizure	Are students entitled to due process before a short suspension? If so, what process is due? What procedural rights do they have before being expelled? What is an adequate notice and hearing? When are they entitled to a lawyer, to bring witnesses, to cross-examine their accuser or to appeal? Is due process different for students in special education? When can students be searched? Can teachers search students' cell phones or backpacks?
5. Student Harassment and Bullying	When can schools be held liable for sexual harassment among students? Do students have to tell teachers or principals about the harassment? Does the harassment have to be severe or pervasive? Do schools have a duty to prevent the harassment? Does the harassment have to be sexual? What about harassment based on religion, race, or sexual orientation? When are schools liable for a teacher's harassment of a student?
6. Teacher Freedom of Expression	Can teachers be punished for publicly criticizing school policy or for complaining about working conditions? Do whistle-blower laws protect teachers? Do teachers have a right to use controversial materials or methods in class? Do they have a right to express their personal views about political or social questions in response to student questions?
7. Teacher Out-of-School Conduct	Can administrators discipline teachers for immoral or unprofessional conduct away from school? What constitutes immoral or unprofessional conduct? Can teachers date students if they are over 18 and not in their classes? What illegal conduct would justify firing a teacher? Could photos on Facebook get teachers in trouble?

Lesson Plan	Description
8. Religion	Are students allowed to pray before, during, or after school? Must schools recognize student prayer clubs? Are invocations and benedictions permitted at graduation? What about silent prayer or meditation? Are courses that teach about the Bible or religion permitted? Must schools excuse students from reading books or studying topics that violate their religious beliefs? Are Christmas assemblies OK? Do teachers have a right to exclude evolution or include intelligent design in their science curriculum? Can students be required to stand for the Pledge of Allegiance?
9. Student Records: The Family Educational Rights and Privacy Act	Are parents entitled to see all of their child's records? Can parents prohibit outsiders from having access? Are there circumstances that allow the records to be shared without parental consent? Do noncustodial parents have a right to see their child's records? Are parents entitled to a hearing to challenge the accuracy of their child's records or grades? Do teachers have a right to see the records of their students? Can parents sue teachers for putting negative and critical comments in the student's records?
10. Abuse and Neglect	What constitutes abuse or neglect? Are all school staff required to report child abuse? To whom must educators report? Must teachers be sure of abuse before reporting? If an investigation determines that no abuse occurred, could parents sue the reporting teacher for defamation?

HOW TO USE THIS BOOK

We have designed each lesson so that it can be completed in one sixty-minute professional-development session. These are "ready-made" lessons that require a minimum of preparation time for the presenter. We fully realize that this target may not be achievable if the user is seeking a comprehensive understanding of the law for the participants. Therefore, we include a number of alternative ideas and supplemental resources, so users can add to the lessons as they see fit. For example, we provide strategies that ask participants to prepare for the law lesson prior to entry in the professional-development session.

We have designed these lessons around principles of good teaching and learning. However, we strongly encourage the presenters to use ideas from other lessons (e.g., using the motivator strategy in the teacher-freedom-of-expression lesson plan with the content of the religion lesson) or proven strategies from their own professional experience (e.g., group activities that you have found valuable) throughout these lesson plans. Our lessons are divided into the following steps:

1. Activator/Motivator

We agree with John Dewey and many cognitive psychologists that learning occurs through the heart on the way to the mind. As such, we created an anticipatory set—what we call an Activator/Motivator—for each lesson. Each Activator/Motivator is designed to garner the attention of participants and engage their hearts and minds. Each Activator/Motivator can be modified to meet the specific context in your local school setting.

2. Rationale/Objectives

Learners need to know what they are expected to learn. For each lesson, we have identified the purpose and specific goals. Also in each lesson, we suggest that the goals should be posted and stated. However, each facilitator should integrate the goals into the lesson as they see fit.

3. The Law

We provide current, relevant legal content for each lesson. However, this book is not designed as a comprehensive educational-law text. Instead, it provides a summary of the basic legal principles that are most important for teachers to understand. We do not advise that facilitators read the Law section to participants or simply hand out this section for participant review. In order to promote a learner-centered pedagogical approach, we offer a specific teaching and learning strategy for each lesson. Each is designed to be ready to use; however, as with the Motivator/Activator, we encourage facilitators to modify lessons and to replicate pedagogical strategies from other lessons as they see fit.

4. Application/Content to Practice

Principals will use a variety of activities with teachers to help them apply what they learned in the legal-content section to real school issues.

5. Assessment

The big question in any teaching setting is: Did they learn, and can they apply the knowledge? The purpose of this section is to ascertain learning. Finally, as with the other lesson-plan sections, we highly recommend setting (e.g., elementary or secondary) and personal modifications (e.g., emphasizing certain aspects of a lesson).

We also provide additional sections for each lesson:

Questions and Answers

We predict that participants will have additional questions as a result of the lessons. While there is no end to the "What if ..." questions, we provide a list of questions teachers are likely to ask. The questions can also be integrated into many aspects of each lesson, including the Motivator/Activator, the Law, or the Assessment.

Resources/Materials

We have provided a set of resources, materials, and references at the end of each chapter.

Relevant Quotes

Historical and/or precedent-setting quotes and cases are highlighted. These can be used for multiple purposes in different parts of the lesson plans.

Materials

All the material needed to conduct each lesson will be listed for each lesson. YouTube clips may need to be downloaded to your computer in order to be accessed in a meeting without Internet connectivity. Also, if a YouTube clip is no longer available, we encourage principals to search on YouTube for other relevant clips.

References

A list of readily available references will be provided. Rather than a comprehensive list, we identify specific chapters of popular school-law texts that can be used to augment each lesson.

Icons

We use a selection of icons throughout the book to guide the facilitators for portions of the lesson plan. Below are the elements of our lesson plans. Throughout each chapter, you will see icons as you flow through the various elements of the lesson plan.

We provide three icons to assist the facilitator. The first is a **clock** that signifies the *amount of time* that should be spent on each section in order to complete the lesson in sixty minutes. The second is a **stack of paper**, which will signify that the following content can be used as a handout. Finally, the **star** icon will be used to highlight a *supplemental activity*.

- **Clock icon:**

- **Handout icon:**

- **Supplemental Activity icon:**

Rowman & Littlefield has made the handouts included in this book available as a single PDF formatted for easy and clear printing on 8.5″ × 11″ paper. To acquire a copy of the PDF version of these resources, please visit the http://rowman.com/ISBN/9781475831184/Principals-Avoiding-Lawsuits and click on the "Features" tab to download the PDF.

CAUTIONARY NOTE

It is important to acknowledge two important issues associated with the delivery of the school-law lesson plans. First, we fully understand the difficulty of teaching, especially teaching adult learners. That is to say, any presentation can easily go astray with "But, what if ..." questions. We anticipate that many teachers may want to debate the merits, realities, or "correctness" of the law discussed in these lessons.

If facilitators are restricted to sixty-minutes sessions, they need to stress that these lessons are not designed as a debate, but rather to present what educators need to know to protect themselves and their schools so they are not inhibited by misinformation. Facilitators should anticipate this and, if possible, build in a small amount of time (preferably before the lesson) for participants to opine about the law itself.

Second, although we believe this book is accurate at the time of publication, it is not intended to be used as legal advice for anyone facing or contemplating litigation. Because the law is constantly changing and varies among the states, educators considering legal action should not rely on this book. Instead, they should consult with a knowledgeable lawyer and/or their professional association. As litigation is often an unhappy, expensive, difficult and time-consuming experience, going to court should usually be a last resort. Therefore, we hope this book will enable teachers and principals to resolve disputes through discussion, negotiation, and education in order to avoid lawsuits.

REQUEST TO USERS

This is a pioneering book. We believe it is the first of its kind, and we want it to work for you and your teachers. By sending us your comments and suggestions, you can help us improve the next edition. What did you find useful? What should be added or eliminated? What was confusing or unclear? Please send your comments and suggestions to David Schimmel, University of Massachusetts (schimmel200@gmail.com); Suzanne Eckes, Indiana University (seckes@indiana.edu); and Matthew Militello, East Carolina University (militellom14@ecu.edu).

Thanks from each of us.

REFERENCES

Dewey, J. (1902). *The child and curriculum*. Chicago: University of Chicago Press.
Schimmel, D., & Militello, M. (2007). Legal literacy for teachers: A neglected responsibility. *Harvard Educational Review*, 77(2), 257–284.

Chapter One

Liability for Student Injuries

Protecting Your Teachers, Your Students, and Your School

BACKGROUND

Probably no area of school law arouses more anxiety, confusion, and misunderstanding than the possibility of being sued for student injury. Rumors circulate in many teachers' rooms about educators who have lost their job and their life's savings because some injured student won a million-dollar award against them. As a result of the possibility of being sued, many educators view the law as an invisible monster hiding in every classroom, hallway, and playground ready to ensnare any teacher who makes an innocent mistake. Thus there emerges a sense that teaching is an especially dangerous profession in which hazards are greater, liability is more personal, negligence more likely and the result of negligence more disastrous for educators than other people. One result of this erroneous perception is that many teachers fail to discipline students when they should because of unfounded fear of being sued. Similarly, some teachers don't intervene in fights when they may, or if they do, they worry unnecessarily about being sued if a student is injured.

This lesson will clarify many of these confusions and misunderstandings. It will outline what an injured student has to prove to hold teachers or schools liable for their injuries. One outcome of this lesson is that it will enable teachers and administrators to have a common understanding of the law that applies to student injuries and would enable them to collaborate in practicing preventive law. As practitioners of preventive law, they will be able to protect themselves, their students, and their schools.

Activator

Motivator

5 Minutes

In this activity ask participants to indicate whether they think educators can be held liable for student injuries in a number of hypothetical cases. Distribute copies of the following table and ask teachers to indicate whether they believe the teacher in each case would be held liable or not. If you choose, you may tally totals for each response and write the number in each column. Finally, tell participants that you will return to these cases later in the lesson and transition into the rationale and goals of the lesson.

Handout 1.1   Student Injury Hypothetical Cases

Hypothetical Cases	Is the Teacher Liable?		
CASE #1: As a result of Mr. Big's use of reasonable force to break up a fight in the hallway, one of the students hits his head on the floor and has a serious concussion.	Yes	No	Don't Know
Totals			
CASE #2: After an evening play rehearsal, Mrs. Care gives a student a ride home without parental permission, and the student is injured, but not because of the teacher's negligence.	Yes	No	Don't Know
Totals			
CASE #3: Although Mr. Carefree is supposed to be on duty in the gym at 1:00 p.m., he drinks another cup of coffee in the teachers' room and then walks into the gym at 1:15. At 1:14, a high school student is seriously injured when he bumps heads with a classmate while jumping for a rebound during a friendly basketball game.	Yes	No	Don't Know
Totals			
CASE #4: Miss Busy leaves her class for 10 minutes to duplicate science worksheets. She tells the students to work quietly while she is gone. When she leaves, some students begin to throw spitballs, pencils, and paper planes. After seven or eight minutes, a girl is struck by a pencil and blinded in one eye.	Yes	No	Don't Know
Totals			
CASE #5: As the bus was leaving the high school on a field trip, 16-year-old Flo Friendly suddenly reached out of the window to wave at a friend and broke her arm when it hit a lamppost. She sued teacher Tripper for failing to adequately supervise and for not warning students not to open the bus windows.	Yes	No	Don't Know
Totals			

Hypothetical Cases	Is the Teacher Liable?		
CASE #6: Instead of paying attention to the students when she was on playground duty, Mrs. Lesscare was gossiping with another teacher. During this time, Sue Sadly ran across the playground, tripped, fell on her face, broke three teeth, and received six stitches.	Yes	No	Don't Know
Totals			
CASE #7: Despite repeated warnings to Bob Bobbing to stay in his seat, he continued to jump out of his seat, disrupt the class, and perhaps injure himself. As a result, teacher Strictman puts a restraining hand on Bob's shoulder against the advice of a colleague who told him, "Never touch a student."	Yes	No	Don't Know
Totals			

Consider sending the scenarios out beforehand. That way you can ask teachers to complete all of the scenarios without taking time out of the lesson.

Rationale

5 Minutes

Because there is widespread fear of being held liable for student injury (which may inhibit appropriate disciplinary action) and because of extensive misunderstanding about how the law applies to these situations, it is important for teachers to understand when and why educators can and cannot be held personally liable.

Objectives

Post and/or state the following objectives for the lesson plan:

1. Teachers will understand what an injured student must prove in order to hold teachers and/or schools liable.
2. Teachers will be able to apply the "reasonably prudent teacher" standard in order to "practice preventive law."
3. Teachers will become familiar with how insurance as well as state and federal laws might protect educators from personal liability.

The Law

15 Minutes

In this section of the lesson plan the principal will provide the content needed for educators to make informed and legal decisions. This lesson is based on the law of torts. Torts are civil (as contrasted with criminal) wrongs and are primarily an area of state law, rather than law made by the federal government. Tort law imposes a duty of care on educators. This means that educators must use reasonable care not to injure their students and to protect their students from foreseeable dangers.

If educators fail to use reasonable care, they are considered negligent. If their negligence is the cause of a student's injury, they or their school may be held liable in money damages to compensate the student for his or her injuries. To determine whether an educator is negligent, courts ask if he or she acted as a reasonably prudent teacher (RPT) should have acted under the circumstances. If in doubt about how an RPT should act, a teacher should consult with prudent, experienced teachers and/or administrators who have faced similar circumstances.

In considering whether to hold teachers and/or schools liable for a student's injuries, judges would apply the above principles and ask four questions. (Use the handout/presentation slide below to provide the law for each of these questions.)

Handout 1.2   Student Injury Liability Questions

Questions	The Law
1. Was there a duty of care?	Educators have a duty not to injure their students and to protect them from known or foreseeable dangers.
2. Was there negligence?	Teachers are negligent when they fail to act as a hypothetical *reasonably prudent teacher* (RPT) should have acted under the circumstances. To determine whether a teacher acted as an RPT, the teacher's behavior is measured against the professional norms of prudent teachers. If they do act as an RPT under the circumstances, they are not negligent. When circumstances are more dangerous (e.g., on field trips, in chemistry class, or when working with young children), a reasonably prudent teacher should provide clearer warnings and closer supervision.
3. Did the negligence cause the injury?	The plaintiff (or injured student) must prove not only that the defendant teacher who is being sued is negligent but also that the negligence caused the injury. (Plaintiffs usually sue for a dollar amount for medical expenses, lost wages, and/or pain and suffering to compensate them for their injury.)
4. Was there contributory negligence?	Adults and most high school students are expected to exercise ordinary/reasonable care and not to expose themselves to known or obvious dangers. Therefore, in most states, if an injured person's own negligence contributed to her injury, courts would usually reduce the amount of the dollar award to the injured person in proportion to her negligence. This is known as *comparative negligence*. For example, an older student might have her award reduced by 40% if the judge concluded that she was 40% responsible for her own injury. However, if she was primarily responsible for her injury (i.e., more than 50%), she would probably receive no award.
	In all states different standards apply to children. Generally, children under the age of seven cannot be charged with contributory negligence. Children between 7 and 14 are presumed incapable of contributory negligence. And beyond the age of 14, students are expected to act as reasonably prudent students of their age and maturity should act under the circumstances.

Consider providing teachers with a blank note sheet with the four questions (from Handout 1.2). Ask the teachers to take notes as you deliver the content.

To summarize, the legal principles relevant to student injury—that educators have a duty to act with reasonable care, that they are negligent if they fail to do so, and that they can be held liable if their negligence causes injury. The principles are relatively easy to understand, and with practice in applying them, teachers and principals can anticipate and prevent problems that can lead to lawsuits.

Although there is little chance of RPTs being held personally liable for student injuries, this fact should not make competent teachers less careful. Instead, this knowledge should:

1. Reduce misinformation and misunderstanding about teacher liability;
2. Enable teachers to enforce reasonable discipline and order without unfounded fear; and
3. Enable teachers to collaborate with their principals and colleagues in applying the "reasonably prudent teacher" standard to issues of supervision and safety. As a result of this knowledge, teachers will be less likely to view law as a source of anxiety, and instead feel empowered to be practitioners of preventive law when confronting legal issues.

Application/Content to Practice

15 Minutes

Divide the participants into small groups of three to five and ask them to take out the hypothetical cases they used in the Activator/ Motivator. The goal is to determine whether it is likely that the teachers in the scenarios would or would not be held liable by applying the principles we have explained to the facts of the cases. That is, in each case ask:

Handout 1.3 Questions about the Hypothetical Cases

1. Was there a duty of care?
2. Was the teacher negligent (i.e., did the teacher fail to act as a reasonably prudent teacher should have under the circumstances)?
3. Did the teacher's negligence cause the injury?
4. If so, was there contributory negligence that might reduce the award to the plaintiff?

After the small groups report the results of their discussion of the cases, the principal can use the following answers to summarize and clarify how the principles of law would likely apply. The principal may need to address only selective cases as time permits.

Handout 1.4   Results for Hypothetical Cases

Case	Result
Case #1	TEACHER NOT LIABLE. Mr. Big has a duty to protect students from being injured. If, pursuant to that duty, he tries to break up a fight, and he unintentionally injures a student, he should not be held liable for the student's injury. This is because a teacher who uses reasonable force to protect himself or a student is not negligent even if a student is injured in the process. Furthermore, even if the teacher were negligent, many state laws and the federal Teacher Liability Protection Act (2001) would probably protect him from liability if his action was carried out to "maintain order or control in the classroom."
Case #2	Mrs. Care is NOT LIABLE for the student's injuries if they were not caused by her negligence. The fact that Mrs. Care did not have a parent's permission may or may not have violated a school policy. But even if Mrs. Care did violate school policy (or administrative advice), this would not make her a negligent driver, and if she was not negligent, she cannot be held liable for the student's injury.
Case #3	In this case, Mr. Carefree is NOT LIABLE for the student's injury. By drinking coffee when he should have been supervising the gym, Mr. Carefree was negligent and violated his contractual duties. But if bumping heads in a friendly game is an accident that would not have been prevented even if a reasonably prudent teacher would have been present, then Carefree would not be liable for the injury because his negligent absence was not the cause of the accident. Carefree should be disciplined for not being on duty when he should have been supervising the students. But he could only be held liable if the facts of the case were different, and the injured student could prove that a reasonable teacher's presence would have prevented the injury.
Case #4	Miss Busy probably is LIABLE for the injury of the blinded student. Miss Busy had a duty to protect her students from injuries caused by other students when such injuries could have been prevented by reasonable supervision. If, under the circumstances of this case, a reasonably prudent teacher would not have left the classroom unattended for 10 minutes, then Busy was negligent for doing so. And if a reasonably careful teacher would have stopped the students' misconduct before it caused the injury, then a judge or jury could conclude that Busy's negligence caused the injury.
Case #5	In this case Mr. Tripper probably would NOT be held liable since a judge or jury would probably conclude that Miss Friendly was negligent in failing to act as a reasonably prudent high school student should have under the circumstances. High school students have a duty to exercise ordinary care and not to expose themselves to obvious dangers. Even if Mr. Tripper was not watching Miss Friendly when she suddenly reached out of the bus, her negligent behavior was the primary cause of the injury—not the action or inaction of Mr. Tripper.
Case #6	Probably NOT LIABLE. Mrs. Lesscare was negligent for not paying attention to the students when she was on playground duty, and perhaps she should be disciplined for her failure to carry out her duty of care. But she could not be liable for the injury to Sue (which was an accident that was caused by her running) if Sue's injury would not have been prevented if Lesscare was carefully supervising and not gossiping.

Case	Result
Case #7	Probably NOT LIABLE. Mr. Strictman may have ignored the advice of his colleagues, but this does not mean he could be held liable for preventing Bob from repeatedly jumping out of his seat, disrupting the class, and possibly injuring himself. Although many educators tell teachers, "Never touch a student," this is overly broad advice and in some situations is poor advice. Certainly sexual touches of students by teachers are always illegal. But there are many situations where the law permits teachers to use reasonable force to protect themselves or their students and use reasonable restraint to enforce discipline. In fact, the purpose of the Teacher Liability Protection Act is to protect teachers from frivolous lawsuits and the fear of liability for their reasonable actions to maintain order in their classrooms.

Assessment

10 Minutes

One way to assess student understanding is to ask them to apply the legal principles they learned to the following variations of the cases we have discussed. Copy the two scenarios below and fold each on the dotted line. Ask participants to read only the question portion of question number 1. Ask participants to pair up and discuss what they each think about the scenario. After a few minutes inform the pairs to open their cards and review the answer. Repeat this with the second scenario.

Handout 1.5   Liability Assessment Scenarios

Q1. While Mr. Carefree was having coffee instead of supervising the gym, some of the students started a rough basketball game that included pushing, elbowing, and cursing. After 10 minutes of increasingly unsportsmanlike conduct, one of the students intentionally tripped another player, who was seriously injured just as Mr. Carefree entered the gym. Is the teacher liable? Why or why not?
A1. Mr. Carefree probably would be held liable because he was negligent in not being on duty in the gym and because a reasonably prudent teacher would have intervened to stop the uncontrolled game before the student was injured.
Q2. Just before Miss Busy returned to her classroom after duplicating worksheets for 10 minutes, a student threw a baseball from the playground that shattered a window and sprayed glass that blinded one student's eye. Is the teacher liable?
A2. Miss Busy would not be held liable because the presence of a prudent teacher would not have prevented the unforeseeable injury that occurred.

FAQ

10 Minutes

As time permits, you may add some of these additional questions to the follow-up discussion.

Handout 1.6   Additional Liability Questions and Answers

1. **What should teachers do when they confront new situations that might pose dangers such as field trips?**
   When in doubt about what one's duty of care requires, a reasonably prudent teacher should CONSULT with other prudent teachers or administrators who have confronted similar situations. By collaboratively developing and following safety checklists, teachers protect their students, themselves, and their schools.

2. **Are teachers liable for ANY injury that occurs if they leave their classroom unattended?**
   No. There may be emergencies in or outside the classroom that would require a reasonably prudent teacher to *briefly* leave her class, and in these circumstances, she would not be negligent for doing so.

3. **Can teachers be held liable for failing to prevent every injury that might occur when they are supervising a class, hallway, or playground?**
   No. Most injuries are caused by accidents which are not the result of anyone's negligence and for which no one is liable. Furthermore, teachers cannot be expected to anticipate every situation in which one student could injure another. The law does not expect teachers to prevent unforeseeable injuries, only those that ordinary care can prevent.

4. **Do teachers have a duty to physically intervene in a fight?**
   Not necessarily. It depends on the circumstances. For example, a female teacher has no duty to physically intervene in a fist-fight between two high school students and risk injury. In many situations, teachers simply have the duty to seek help when circumstances are beyond their control.

5. **What happens if I am injured while breaking up a student fight?**
   Teachers would likely be covered by their medical insurance for short- and long-term disability as well as workman's compensation for a serious injury.

6. **If parents sign waivers, does that protect teachers and schools from liability?**
   Not necessarily. In many states, courts construe such waivers very strictly or rule that waivers of responsibility in school activities are against public policy. In a few states, such as Massachusetts, courts uphold waivers in extracurricular activities—especially those that students and parents know are dangerous. Although it is usually wise to ask parents to sign permission slips to permit their children to participate in special activities, parents should not be asked to waive their right to sue educators who are negligent and whose negligence causes student injuries because most courts are not likely to uphold such waivers and because parents should not be asked to waive their children's rights.

7. **If a teacher's negligence causes an injury, would s/he be personally liable or do teachers have any protections?**
   Teachers who belong to organizations such as the National Education Association (NEA) or the American Federation of Teachers are provided with liability insurance (usually for $1,000,0000) as part of their union dues for negligence claims that might be made against them. This policy costs the NEA less than $5 per year to insure each member. Since the premium is based on the likelihood of being sued, this indicates that the chances of a teacher being held liable for a student's injury are extremely low. Also, many school districts and professional associations provide liability insurance for their employees. In addition, many state laws protect public employees such as teachers and principals from being held personally liable for their negligence that occurs within the scope of their employment.

8. **What would happen if a student assaulted a teacher?**
   The student would be subject to school discipline and/or criminal punishment. Although teachers could sue students for damages, this is not likely since even if teachers win their suit, they would be unlikely to collect damages. This is because very few students have independent wealth and because parents usually are not financially responsible for their children's misbehavior.

Consider sending a few of these questions to teachers via e-mail, electronic discussion board, or a hardcopy in their mailbox. Responses can be collected or discussed at the next professional development session.

Resources/Materials

Related Cases

When parents sue schools seeking damages for injuries to their children, they often allege that the injuries were caused by negligent supervision. Whether the supervision was or was not negligent depends on the specific facts of each case. The decisions below illustrate how some courts have ruled on such cases.

- In Louisiana, an elementary student was injured by a classmate with a stick while waiting for the school bus. Parents alleged negligent supervision. But a court ruled that careful supervision would not have prevented the injury. "How," wrote the judge, "could any teacher anticipate a situation where one child, while teasing another child, would be struck in the eye with a stick by a third child?" (*Nash v. Rapides Parish School District*, 1966).
- In another elementary school case, a school was found liable for negligent supervision when a six-year-old student was injured by clearly defective playground equipment. At the time of the injury, about 170 children in the school yard were under the supervision of one teacher whose duties also included helping supervise unloading the school buses. Such supervision, wrote the judge, was "totally inadequate and virtually impossible" (*Gibbins v. Orleans Parish School District*, 1980).
- In California, a district was not held liable for the fatal injury of a 12-year-old student playing a dangerous skateboard game on a school playground at 5:30 p.m. The parents sued for negligent supervision and for not locking up the playground. But the judge ruled that the school's duty of supervision is limited to activities during school hours and to school-related functions and that "prison-tight security for school premises" is not required (*Bartell v. Palos Verdes Peninsula School District*, 1978).

Relevant Quotes

It is the duty of a school to use ordinary care and to prevent students from injury resulting from the conduct of other students under circumstances where such conduct would reasonably have been foreseen and could have been prevented by the use of ordinary care. There is no requirement of constant supervision of all the movements of pupils at all times…. Children have a known proclivity to act impulsively…. It is precisely this lack of mature judgment which makes supervision so vital. The mere presence of the hand of authority and discipline normally is effective to curb this youthful exuberance and to protect children against their own folly.

—*Sheehan v. St. Peters Catholic School* (1971)

As is often the case, accidents … involving school children at play happen so quickly that unless there was direct supervision of every child (which we recognize as being impossible), the accident can be said to be almost impossible to prevent.

—*Nash v. Rapides Parish School Board* (1975)

Clarifying and limiting the liability of teachers, principals and other school professionals who undertake reasonable actions to maintain order, discipline and an appropriate educational environment is an appropriate subject of federal legislation because the scope of the problems created by the legitimate fears of teachers, principals and other school professionals about frivolous, arbitrary or capricious lawsuits against teachers is of national importance ... no teacher in a school shall be liable for harm caused by an act or omission of the teacher on behalf of the school if the actions of the teacher were carried out ... to control, discipline, expel, or suspend a student or maintain order or control in the classroom or school if ... the harm was not caused by willful or criminal conduct, gross negligence [or] reckless misconduct.

—Paul D. Coverdell Teacher Liability Protection Act (2001)

REFERENCES

Bartell v. Palos Verdes Peninsula School District, 147 Cal. Rptr. 898 (1978).
Gibbins v. Orleans Parish School District, 391 So.2d 976 (La. 1980).
Nash v. Rapides Parish School District, 188 So.2d 508 (La. 1975).
Sheehan v. St. Peters Catholic School, 188 N.W.2d 868 (Minn. 1971).

ADDITIONAL RESOURCES

Alexander, K., & Alexander, M. D. (2011). *American public school law* (8th ed.). Belmont, CA: Wadsworth (See chapter 11).

Schimmel, D., Stellman, L., Conlon, C., & Fischer, L. (2015). *Teachers and the law* (9th ed.). Boston: Allyn and Bacon (See chapter 5).

Russo, C. (2009). *Reutter's the law of public education* (7th ed.). New York: Foundation Press (See chapter 8).

Teacher Liability Protection Act, 20 U.S.C. 6731–6769 (2001).

McCarthy, M., Cambron-McCabe, N., & Eckes, S. (2015). *Public school law: Teachers' and students' rights* (7th ed.). Boston: Allyn and Bacon (See chapter 13).

Chapter Two

Student Freedom of Expression

BACKGROUND

There is much debate involving students' rights to freedom of expression in public schools. For example, can students be punished for sending harassing messages to classmates from their home computer? Or is it permissible for a student to wear a confederate flag T-shirt or one that includes homophobic speech?

Before the 1960s, there was little hope that courts would strike down school rules that restricted student freedom of speech. As a practical matter, the First Amendment did not apply to public schools. This is because courts used a "reasonableness" test to judge school policies. This meant that rules were upheld unless students could prove that they were not reasonable. Since administrators could almost always articulate some reason to justify their rules, restrictions on student speech were almost always upheld.

This changed in 1969 when the U.S. Supreme Court handed down a landmark decision in the case of *Tinker v. Des Moines* that replaced the reasonableness test. In *Tinker*, the Court ruled that the First Amendment applied to students in the public schools and that restrictions on student speech were unconstitutional unless schools had evidence that the expression would cause substantial disruption or interfere with the rights of others.

In the years that followed, the Supreme Court ruled on three other student speech cases that clarified the scope and limits of *Tinker*. In 1986, the Court held that lewd and indecent speech is not protected by the First Amendment in public schools. In 1988, the Court ruled on a school newspaper case and established guidelines on when educators can control school-sponsored student expression. And in 2007, the Court explained that schools could restrict student speech that promoted illegal behavior.

These four Supreme Court cases form the constitutional context for today's many controversies about student expression. They also have been applied in cases involving student's off-campus Internet speech.

This lesson will help teachers understand the principles that emerge from these Court decisions. It also will help them understand when they can and cannot restrict controversial expressions in school and in offensive websites, e-mail messages, and other emerging social media outlets.

Activator

Motivator

5 Minutes

Distribute copies of the following table and ask teachers to indicate if they believe that schools violated student freedom of expression in each of the cases. If you choose, you may tally responses by all participants and post the totals on a slide or overhead. Finally, tell participants that you will return to these cases later in the lesson and transition into the goals of the lesson.

You might enhance the motivator by distributing 3 × 5 cards that say "VIOLATION" on one side and "NO VIOLATION" on the other side. (*Note*: This can also be accomplished with color-coded cards. For instance, green would indicate no violation and red may indicate a violation.) As a group, read each case and ask participants to hold up the card that best expresses their understanding of the issue.

Handout 2.1   Student Freedom of Expression Hypothetical Cases

Hypothetical Cases	Did Schools Violate Student Freedom of Expression?		
1. Students in Yourtown Middle School were prohibited from wearing buttons with a red slash through a swastika and the wording "NO SCHOOL UNIFORMS" to protest the new policy requiring all students to wear uniforms. Administrators felt that the buttons with the swastikas were offensive.	They Did	They Did Not	Don't Know
2. In a high school journalism course that publishes *Spectrum*, the school newspaper, editor Veritas Strong wrote an editorial criticizing one of the candidates for the local school board. The journalism teacher censored Strong's editorial based on his policy of "keeping our schools out of local school politics."	They Did	They Did Not	Don't Know
3. As a joke, J.S. created a fake profile making fun of her principal on a social media site. The profile contained juvenile humor and an absurd depiction of the principal as a sex addict. The profile was not viewed at school since the district blocked access to the site. When the principal learned about the profile, he suspended J.S. for 10 days because he said the profile was defamatory and offensive. J.S. argued that the suspension violated her free speech rights because there was no evidence that anyone took the profile seriously, and it caused no disruption at school.			

Hypothetical Cases	Did Schools Violate Student Freedom of Expression?		
4. Each year, the student members of the high school drama club selected a popular Broadway musical for their annual show. But this year the faculty adviser, Karol Kaution, rejected the student selection because it included profanity.	They Did	They Did Not	Don't Know
5. A high school student, Calvin Cool, was suspended for refusing to take off a T-shirt that said, "Legalize Pot." The principal explained that if Calvin was allowed to wear the shirt, other students or their parents might think the school was willing to tolerate an illegal activity.	They Did	They Did Not	Don't Know
6. A student, Bob Anger, was suspended for two days because of his home website's "disrespectful" message to other students saying that the school football coach was "lousy" and should be replaced.	They Did	They Did Not	Don't Know
7. A teacher tells Henry Patrick that he may not be required to say the Pledge of Allegiance, but he must stand "in respectful silence." Henry is suspended when he refuses to stand.	They Did	They Did Not	Don't Know
8. A high school student, Kara K., used her home computer to create a discussion group on a social media site, and invited 100 "friends" to join. The discussion focused on Shay, a student who was accused of having herpes and being a slut. After Shay complained to school officials, Kara was given a 10-day suspension. But Kara argued that the suspension violated her First Amendment rights because the discussion occurred off-campus and had not caused any disruption in school. Administrators justified the suspension because the web page violated the school's antiharassment policy and because there was evidence that it was "foreseeable" that Kara's web page would cause disruption at school.	They Did	They Did No	Don't Know
9. Teacher Ron Respekt ordered a student to take off a "disrespectful" T-shirt that said, "President Obama Is an International Terrorist." Mr. Respekt was concerned that the shirt might lead to conflicts between students who supported American bombing in Iraq and those who opposed our "killing of innocent civilians."	They Did	They Did Not	Don't Know
10. Teacher I.M. Caring prohibited two student T-shirts that were designed to protest the high school's Tolerance Day. One shirt read, "Be Happy, Be Straight"; the other read, "Homosexuals Are Sinful and Shameful."	They Did	They Did Not	Don't Know

Note: Principals can change the names and especially the grade levels when appropriate.

Rationale

5 Minutes

It is important that teachers understand this area of law in order to respond effectively and legally when such issues arise. Discuss with the teachers whether students have a First Amendment right to wear these shirts.

Figure 2.1   Figure 2.2

Figure 2.3   Figure 2.4

Objectives

Post and/or state the following objectives for the lesson plan:

1. Teachers will be able to identify the constitutional principles established by the Supreme Court concerning the scope and limits of student freedom of expression in the public schools.
2. Teachers will be able to apply the reasoning of other federal and state decisions dealing with controversial student expression in their schools.
3. Teachers will be able to apply First Amendment principles and precedents to the kinds of student speech controversies that are likely to arise in the future.

The Law

15 Minutes

Four U.S. Supreme Court decisions have given schools guidance about when they can and cannot restrict student speech. These cases include the principles for understanding the scope and limits of student freedom of speech.

Political Speech: Tinker v. Des Moines *(1969)*

In 1965, students from Des Moines, Iowa, protested against the war in Vietnam by wearing black armbands to school. Since administrators had prohibited the armbands (fearing disruption), they suspended the protesters who took their case to court. In 1969, the U.S. Supreme Court ruled that students do not "shed their constitutional right to freedom of speech or expression at the schoolhouse gate."

The Court explained that schools may not be "enclaves of totalitarianism," and fear of disturbance "is not enough to overcome the right to freedom of expression." Since there was no evidence in this case that the armband wearers interfered with the school's work or the rights of other students, the Court ruled that the armbands were the kind of symbolic speech protected by the First Amendment.

The *Tinker* decision does not mean that schools cannot limit student expression. On the contrary, there are limits to all constitutional rights. Thus the question in this and every case dealing with student expression is: When must schools tolerate and protect, or when can they prohibit and punish controversial speech? In *Tinker*, the Court ruled that schools cannot punish student speech because it is controversial or unpopular. However, schools can prohibit and discipline students if there is evidence that their speech "materially disrupts classwork or involves substantial disorder or invasion of the rights of others."

Lewd and Indecent Speech: Bethel School District v. Fraser *(1986)*

This case arose when Matthew Fraser gave a nominating speech at a high school assembly that used an elaborate, graphic sexual metaphor to refer to his candidate. In this case, the Supreme Court ruled that the First Amendment does not protect student speech that is "offensively lewd and indecent" in school-sponsored activities even if it does not cause substantial disruption. Furthermore, the Court held that school officials have discretion to determine "what manner of speech" is vulgar and lewd in classrooms and school-sponsored activities.

School-Sponsored Speech: Hazelwood School District v. Kuhlmeier *(1988)*

In Hazelwood High School, the principal censored two stories from the school newspaper that was published by the Journalism II class. The principal deleted the stories to protect the privacy of the students and parents involved in the articles, and the Supreme Court ruled in his favor.

The Court explained that educators can control curricular-related publications, school plays, and other school-sponsored activities that "bear the imprimatur" (i.e., officially approved by) of the school. This is because the school as publisher of a newspaper or producer of a play "may refuse to lend its name and resources" to student expression that does not meet its standards. In short, the Court ruled that educators do not violate the First Amendment by "exercising editorial control over the style and content of student speech in school-sponsored expressive activities so long as their actions are reasonably related to legitimate pedagogical concerns."

Advocating Illegal Activities: Morse v. Frederick *(2007)*

Joseph Frederick was suspended after displaying a banner that read "BONG HITS 4 JESUS" at a school-sponsored event on a street in front of his high school when the Olympic torch passed by. School administrators thought the banner encouraged drug use in violation of school policy. A majority of the Supreme Court agreed that the school could restrict Frederick's banner because schools can prohibit student expression that "they reasonably regard as promoting illegal drug use."

Some of the justices emphasized that this decision was consistent with *Tinker* and did not mean that schools could restrict student views just because they were offensive or were in conflict with the school's stated mission. Nor did *Morse* support any restriction on student speech "commenting on any political or social issue." Although *Morse* was a narrow decision that only applied to promoting illegal drug use, it is likely that it will allow schools to also restrict the direct promotion of other illegal activities.

In sum, these four decisions identified the scope and limits of student freedom of expression in public schools. *Tinker* ruled that the First Amendment does protect students' individual expression even if it is controversial, offensive, or unpopular. But *Tinker* also recognized two limitations: speech that caused substantial disruption or interfered with the rights of others. The three subsequent cases added three other limitations. *Bethel* excluded from First Amendment protection vulgar and lewd speech in school-related activities. *Hazelwood* excluded from protection curriculum and activities that were directly sponsored by and identified with the school. And *Morse* excluded student expression that promoted illegal activities.

Use the handouts/presentation slides below to guide the discussion.

Handout 2.2   Student Freedom of Expression Slides/Handouts

Slide 1: Political Speech *Tinker v. Des Moines* (1969) When must schools tolerate and protect and when can they prohibit or punish controversial speech?
Slide 2: Lewd and Indecent Speech *Bethel School District v. Fraser* (1986) Can schools prohibit vulgar and lewd speech if it doesn't cause a disruption?
Slide 3: School-Sponsored Speech *Hazelwood School District v. Kuhlmeier* (1988) When can schools control student newspapers or plays?
Slide 4: Advocating Illegal Activities *Morse v. Frederick* (2007) Can schools punish students who advocate illegal activity?

Divide participants into four groups. Create handouts from the information provided for each case and ask each group to answer one or two of the following questions:

1. When must schools tolerate and protect and when can they prohibit or punish controversial speech?
2. Can schools prohibit vulgar and lewd speech if it doesn't cause a disruption?
3. When can schools control student newspapers or plays?
4. Can schools punish students who advocate illegal activity?

Ask the groups to consider how these might relate to their school and report out their answers to the larger group.

Application/Content to Practice

15 Minutes

Assign each member within the groups a role: a plaintiff, a defendant, a jury member, and a judge. Then ask the groups to revisit the hypothetical cases used to begin the lesson. Give the defendants and plaintiffs a few minutes to make arguments for or against the hypothetical cases. The jury can then weigh in regarding who made the most convincing argument. Finally, the judge will reveal the answer (provided by the principal, see handout 2.3).

Handout 2.3   Case Scenario Outcomes

Case 1. VIOLATION. Because this is a case of symbolic speech, the principles of *Tinker* apply. According to *Tinker*, students do not shed their constitutional rights to freedom of expression when they enter the public schools unless their expression causes substantial disruption or interferes with the rights of others. In this case, even if the buttons did offend some teachers and administrators, there was no evidence that they caused disruption or interfered with the rights of other students. Therefore, the students had a right to wear their buttons to protest the school's uniform policy, and the school's prohibition of their buttons was unconstitutional.

Case 2. NO VIOLATION. This is a controversy about curriculum-related student expression. Therefore, the principles of the *Hazelwood* case apply. Because the newspaper was published by the students as part of a journalism course under the direction and supervision of the teacher, he had broad authority to decide what topics should and should not be discussed. Most students and some teachers might think that students should be able to discuss local politics in the school paper. But as long as the teacher had some legitimate reason for his decision, students have no constitutional right to challenge his judgment.

In contrast, if *Spectrum* were an "underground" paper published by Veritas in her home, then *Tinker* would apply, and school staff would not be able to prevent her from distributing her article criticizing a school board candidate as long as it didn't cause substantial disruption. Schools can issue reasonable rules concerning the time, place, and manner governing student distribution of non-school-sponsored publications, but distribution can't be prohibited just because the student's views are controversial or offensive. Similarly, *Tinker* applies to students' online publications or blogs that are created on their home computers and are distributed to their friends or classmates.

Case 3. VIOLATION. Applying the principles of *Tinker*, a federal appeals court ruled that the school could not punish J.S. for her speech because it was created off campus, was not viewed on campus, and did not cause disruption. In addition, it was not defamatory because it was "so outrageous" that no one took it seriously, and therefore it did not injure the principal's reputation.

In contrast, a court upheld the punishment of a student who created a false social media site profile of his principal indicating he had inappropriate behavior with his students. This constituted defamation because those who visited the fraudulent website—including parents and a reporter—believed it was authentic and that the principal had been guilty of improper behavior.

Case 4. NO VIOLATION. Here the principles of both *Bethel* and *Hazelwood* apply. In *Bethel*, the Court ruled that the First Amendment does not protect lewd or vulgar speech in a school-related activity even if it does not cause a disruption. Also, the Court allowed educators to decide what speech they consider lewd or vulgar. As the school play is a school-sponsored activity, the faculty advisor had the authority to reject the students' selection of a musical or play that included profanity, and therefore Kaution's decision did not violate the student's free speech rights. In addition, the principles of *Hazelwood*, which give educators broad discretion to control school-sponsored activities, would also lead a court to rule in favor of the school.

Case 5. VIOLATION. This is a controversy where the principles of both *Tinker* and *Morse v. Frederick* apply. In *Morse* the Court ruled that schools could prohibit and punish student speech that promoted illegal drug use. But the Court also reaffirmed *Tinker*'s protection for speech concerning social and/or political messages that did not cause disruption. If the T-shirt had said, "Smoke Pot," school officials would have been able to require the student to take it off because it clearly promoted illegal drugs. But in this case, the message is clearly and primarily political and is not advocating any illegal activity. Therefore, the controversial T-shirt should be a protected form of student expression under the principles of *Tinker* and *Morse*.

Case 6. VIOLATION. Here, again, the *Tinker* decision applies. The First Amendment protects Bob Anger's messages that he disseminates to classmates using his home computer. This includes offensive and controversial views about teachers and coaches. Therefore, Bob should not be punished for criticizing school personnel as long as his messages were not defamatory and did not cause substantial disruption at school.

Case 7. VIOLATION. Judges have ruled in favor of students who refuse to stand during the Pledge. Courts reason that schools cannot require students to engage in "implicit expression" by standing respectfully while the Pledge is being recited. Since standing is an integral part of the Pledge ceremony, one judge wrote that standing "can no more be required than the Pledge itself." Therefore, it was unconstitutional to require Henry Patrick to participate in that form of symbolic expression.

Handout 2.3 *(continued)*

Case 8. NO VIOLATION. According to a federal court, the evidence indicated that Kara's conduct "would reach the school via computers, smart phones and other electronic devices" since Kara's "friends" and the target of the harassment were students at the same school. Therefore, the court ruled that the school was authorized to punish Kara "because her speech interfered with the work and discipline of the school" and because her "hate website" violated the school's antiharassment policy.

Case 9. VIOLATION. The *Tinker* decision is directly relevant to this case. Just as the principal in Des Moines couldn't prohibit Mary Beth Tinker from wearing her armband because of fear of disruption, so Mr. Respekt can't order the student to take off his anti-Obama T-shirt because of his concern that the shirt was "offensive" or "might" cause a conflict—unless he had evidence that would enable him to "forecast substantial disruption."

Case 10. The answer depends on the specific facts of the case. The principles of *Tinker* apply to both T-shirts. But it is likely that the shirt that said, "Be Happy, Be Straight," would be protected if it did not cause disruption since it does not target any individual and is not a serious verbal attack against LGBT students. However, a prohibition of the "Homosexuals Are Sinful and Shameful" shirt could be upheld if the judge concluded that it collided with the rights of gay students to be secure and free from verbal assaults—especially where the school had a history of antigay conflicts. Although *Tinker* applies to both shirts, the outcome in cases such as these may depend as much on the specific circumstances of the case as on the wording of the controversial messages.

Assessment

5 Minutes

To assess teachers' understanding, distribute four cards to each teacher (see below). Ask them to review the summary of each case provided and then to write their response on the opposite side that relates to their current practice. You may need to ask teachers, "How might the knowledge of this case impact your practice?"

Handout 2.4   Student Freedom of Expression Summary Cards

Application to Your Own Practice	*Application to Your Own Practice*
Tinker v. Des Moines: The First Amendment protects student freedom of expression in the public schools unless that expression causes substantial disruption or interferes with the rights of other.	*Bethel v. Fraser*: The First Amendment does not protect offensively lewd and vulgar speech in school-related activities.
Application to Your Own Practice	*Application to Your Own Practice*
Hazelwood v. Kuhlmeier: Educators have broad discretion to control school-sponsored, curricular-related activities such as official school newspapers and school plays.	*Morse v. Frederick*: Schools can prohibit student expression that promotes illegal drug use.

FAQ

As time permits, you may add some of these additional questions to the follow-up discussion.

10 Minutes

1. **Does the First Amendment apply to elementary schools?**
   Probably. But it might depend on the facts of the case. A federal court ruled in favor of elementary students who wore "No School Uniform" buttons (*DePinto v. Bayonne Board of Education*, 2007). The judge rejected the school's argument that *Tinker* does not apply to elementary students. However, another judge wrote that "age is a critical factor in student speech cases" and the Supreme Court "has not suggested that fourth-graders have the same free expression rights of high school students." Thus the answer might depend on both the age of the students and the nature of the speech in question.

2. **Is a threat protected speech?**
   Not if it is a "true threat." Such a threat is unprotected if a reasonable person would interpret the statement as a serious expression of an intent to cause harm. Thus a federal court upheld the expulsion of a junior high school student who wrote a letter describing how he would rape and murder a female classmate who broke up with him (*Doe v. Pulaski School District*, 2002). In contrast, a Michigan court ruled against the expulsion of a student who created "Satan's web page" at home "for laughs" that included "people who are cool" and "people who I wish would die." After reviewing the facts of the case, the judge concluded that no reasonable person would think the statements on the website expressed a serious intent to harm anyone.

   [handwritten: What is a true threat?]

3. **Can schools ban distribution of publications that promote religion?**
   No. Schools cannot restrict the distribution of materials by students because of the subject. Thus an appeals court ruled against the policy of an Illinois school district that banned distribution of all religious material in elementary and junior high schools because students might believe it was endorsed by the school. Instead of censorship, the judge suggested that educators teach students that schools do not endorse speech by permitting it and about why we tolerate divergent views (*Hedge v. Waucanda School District*, 1993).

4. **Can schools restrict the use of school computers?** *[handwritten: Property of school]*
   Yes. Schools have broad discretion to impose any reasonable regulations they wish on the use of school computers. For example, they can develop policies to prohibit inappropriate uses such as violation of copyright laws, harassment of students or staff, commercial purposes, or the search for pornographic material. Or they can simply restrict their use for specific academic purposes.

5. **Can schools restrict cell phones?**
   Yes. Schools have authority to prohibit cell phone use that causes disruption or interferes with the rights of others. Or schools can probably prohibit all cell phones in classrooms or even in school. Although there are not yet any reported court decisions on this issue, schools probably have broad discretion to ban cell phones or restrict their use.

6. Does the First Amendment apply to private or parochial schools?

No. The First Amendment only applies to public schools. Its purpose is to prevent the government or government employees such as teachers from restricting freedom of expression. Thus students in nonpublic schools have no First Amendment rights.

7. Does the student handbook give schools additional rights to restrict "inappropriate" speech?

Not usually. If a school's rule states that teachers can censor student speech that they feel is "inappropriate" but does not cause substantial disruption or interfere with the rights of others, that rule is probably unconstitutional. School rules cannot contradict the Constitution.

8. What is considered a substantial disruption?

It is a disruption that substantially interferes with the work of the school or the rights of others. Deciding what constitutes a substantial disruption should be an objective judgment based on evidence. According to *Tinker*, it should not merely be based on "undifferentiated fear or apprehension of disturbance."

9. Must officials wait until disruption has occurred before acting?

No. Schools can restrict student expression when there is evidence that officials can "reasonably forecast" substantial disruption.

Resources/Materials

Related Cases

Over the years a variety of state and federal courts have applied the principles and precedents of the Supreme Court to other student speech controversies. Instructors might want to mention some of these rulings:

- In Pennsylvania, a court upheld the expulsion of a middle school student who posted a website at home that harassed and threatened his algebra teacher and had a profoundly disruptive effect (*J.S. v. Bethlehem Area School District*, 2002).
- A federal court ruled that a principal violated *Tinker* when he prohibited an elementary student from distributing "Jesus loves me" messages on the school sidewalk after school. According to the judge, "the student speech rights announced in *Tinker* inhere in the elementary school context" (*Morgan v. Swanson*, 659 F.3d 359, 2011).
- In a racially tense Kansas school, administrators prohibited student display of symbols or signs of racial conflict such as Black Power or Confederate flags. A federal court upheld the restrictions because in a place of racial tension, a school does not have to wait for disruption to occur before taking action. In that situation, schools can restrict student expression when there is "a reasonable basis for forecasting disruption" (*West v. Derby Unified School District No. 260*, 2000).
- In New Jersey, a court ruled against an "overbroad" school code that prohibited speech that "creates ill will" because that phrase also prohibits "a significant amount of constitutionally protected speech." The fact that an expression causes hurt

feelings, explained the court, does not mean that it is unprotected (*Sypniewski v. Warren Hills Regional Board of Education*, 2003).

- A federal appeals court upheld the suspension of a high school student who sent violent messages from his home via a social media site threatening to shoot people at his school. Applying *Tinker*, the court ruled that threatening shooting qualified as speech that could lead officials to "forecast substantial disruption" or collide with "the rights of other students to be secure" (*Wynar v. Douglas County School District*, 2013).
- In Missouri, a court upheld the right of administrators to prohibit the marching band from playing a song that appeared to advocate drug use. Applying the principles of *Hazelwood*, the judge ruled that prohibiting the school band from playing a song that advocated drug use was related to reasonable educational concerns (*McCann v. Fort Zumwalt School District*, 1999).
- In an Illinois case, a court upheld the right of a student to write a critical editorial in an underground paper (which was not sponsored by the school). Even though the editorial reflected a "disrespectful and tasteless attitude toward authority," that fact did not justify suspending the student for speech that did not cause substantial disruption (*Scoville v. Board of Education of Joliet Township*, 1970).
- A federal appeals court ruled against a student who wore a T-shirt that said "Homosexuality Is Shameful" on one side and "Be Ashamed, Our School Has Embraced What God Has Condemned" on the other. In this case, the school had a history of anti-homosexual comments that had caused a series of altercations on campus. Furthermore, the court explained that the *Tinker* ruling not only excludes disruptive speech from First Amendment protection but also allows schools to restrict speech which "collides with the rights of other students to be secure and to be left alone." According to the court, this means that students have the right to be free from psychological attacks and verbal assaults on their core identities—especially when they are members of minority groups that historically have been subject to verbal attack (*Harper v. Poway Unified School District*, 2006).

Relevant Quotes

> That [school boards] are educating the young for citizenship is reason for scrupulous protection of Constitutional freedoms of the individual, if we are not to strangle the free mind at its source and teach youth to discount important principles of our government as mere platitudes.

> —*West Virginia v. Barnette* (1943)

> Any word spoken in class, in the lunchroom or on the campus that deviates from the views of another person may start an argument or cause a disturbance. But our Constitution says we must take this risk: and our history says that it is this sort of hazardous freedom—this kind of openness—that is the basis of our national strength.

Students in schools as well as out of school are possessed of fundamental rights which the State must respect, just as they themselves must respect their obligations to the State. In our system, students may not be regarded as closed-circuit recipients of only that which the State chooses to communicate.

—*Tinker v. Des Moines Independent School District* (1969)

The undoubted freedom to advocate unpopular and controversial views in schools and classrooms must be balanced against the society's countervailing interest in teaching students the boundaries of socially appropriate behavior.

Surely it is a highly appropriate function of public school education to prohibit the use of vulgar and offensive terms in public discourse ... vulgar speech and lewd conduct is wholly inconsistent with the "fundamental values" of public school education.

—*Bethel School District v. Fraser* (1986)

A school may, in its capacity as publisher of a school newspaper or producer of a school play "disassociate itself" ... from speech that is, for example, ungrammatical, poorly written, inadequately researched, biased or prejudiced, vulgar or profane or unsuitable for immature audiences ... In addition, a school must be able to take into account the emotional maturity of the intended audience in determining whether to disseminate student speech on potentially sensitive topics.

—*Hazelwood School District v. Kuhlmeier* (1988)

Tinker warned that schools may not prohibit student speech because of a mere desire to avoid ... an unpopular viewpoint. The danger here is far more serious and ... extends well beyond an abstract desire to avoid controversy ... It was reasonably viewed as promoting illegal drug use.

—*Morse v. Frederick* (2007)

REFERENCES

Bethel School District No. 403 v. Fraser, 487 U.S. 675 (1986).
Beussink v. Woodland R-IV School District, 30 F.Supp.2d 1175 (1998).
DePinto v. Bayonne Board of Education, 514 F.Supp.2d 633 (2007).
Doe v. Pulaski School District, 306 F.3d 616 (2002).
Harper v. Poway Unified School District, 445 F.3d 1166 (2006).
Hazelwood School District v. Kuhlmeier, 484 U.S. 260 (1988).
Hedge v. Wauconda School District, 9 F.3d 1295 (1993).
J.S. v. Bethlehem Area School District, 757 A.2d 412 (2002).
Mahaffey v. Aldrich, 236 F.Supp.2d 779 (2002).
McCann v. Fort Zumwalt School District, 50 F.Supp.2d 918 (1999).
Morgan v. Swanson, 659 F.3d 359 (2011).
Morse v. Frederick, 551 U.S. 393 (2007).
Scoville v. Board of Education of Joliet Township, 425 F.2d 10 (1970).
Synpiewski v. Warren Hills Regional Board of Education, 307 F.3d 243 (2003).

Tinker v. Des Moines Independent School District, 393 U.S. 503 (1969).
West Virginia v. Barnette, 319 U.S. 624 (1943).
West v. Derby Unified School District No. 260, 206 F.3d 1358 (2000).
Wynar v. Douglas County School District, 728 F.3d 1062 (2013).

ADDITIONAL RESOURCES

Alexander, K., & Alexander, M. D. (2011). *American public school law* (8th ed.). Belmont, CA: Wordsworth (See chapter 8).

McCaarthy, M., Cambron-McCabe, N., & Eckes, S. (2014). *Public school law*. Boston, MA: Allyn and Bacon/Pearson (See chapter 4).

Russo, C. (2009). *Reutter's the law of public education* (7th ed.). New York: Foundation Press (See chapter 14).

Schimmel, D., Stellman, D., Conlon, C., & Fischer, L. (2015). *Teachers and the law* (9th ed.). Boston: Allyn and Bacon/Pearson (See chapter 10).

Chapter Three

Special Education

BACKGROUND

Historically, students with disabilities have experienced widespread exclusion. The students were often educated in separate schools and classrooms. As a result, laws have been passed by Congress to protect individuals with disabilities from discrimination. In 1975, the Education for All Handicapped Children Act created special educational rights for students with disabilities. This law is now known as the Individuals with Disabilities Education Act (IDEA). In addition to this comprehensive law, Section 504 of the Rehabilitation Act of 1973 (Section 504) and the Americans with Disabilities Act (ADA) provide important legal protections for students with disabilities.

Teachers and school administrators consistently rank special education law as a topic that must be understood when working in a public school. These findings are not surprising, as teachers often confront legal issues when working with special needs students. Thus, an understanding of these laws will help teachers better provide for students with disabilities in their classrooms and protect themselves from possible litigation.

Activator

Motivator

5 Minutes

The principal will ask for four volunteers and will assign each teacher volunteer a role. (*Note*: The principal may want to identify and prepare the four teachers prior to this activity.) The teachers will participate in a mock individualized education program (IEP) meeting while reading from a prepared script. Before beginning the mock IEP meeting, the principal should read the background to set the context.

Background

Fred is a student with autism. His mother has been advocating for support services in school. She recently came across Applied Behavior Analysis (ABA) and believes that

Fred's school should adopt this system. The following took place at an IEP meeting that was convened to discuss Fred's goals for the upcoming academic year.

Special Education Teacher: Thank you for coming to this IEP meeting to discuss Fred's goals. Based on Fred's most recent evaluation, we have decided to continue to provide Fred with support in his classes as well as some pull out support.

Parent: Have you all heard about ABA?

General Teacher: No, what is that?

Principal: Perhaps we should continue with our discussion about Fred's goals.

Parent: (*Ignoring the principal*) ABA is a process called Applied Behavior Analysis. I found an organization on-line that provides training and support for schools. They say it works very well with students like Fred because it helps decrease behavioral problems.

Special Education Teacher: I have heard of it, but it was not part of our professional development this past year or this coming summer.

Parent: I'd like Fred to be in a program like this.

Teacher: Well, I think it's a good idea, but to start a new program at this time of the year could compromise my ability to provide for all children in my classroom. I'm worried that I just won't have the time to do ABA "right" and meet everyone else's needs.

Principal: Our district doesn't have the human resources to sponsor individual therapy for students. I have complete confidence in our faculty and the program we provide to all our special education students.

Occupational Therapist: There is not conclusive evidence that ABA works with children. If this program isn't "research based," we shouldn't be using it.

After the meeting Fred's mom said to the special education teacher, "I don't know, I am confused. If this is something that would help Fred why won't the school get the program? What can I do if I think Fred is not getting the programming he needs?"

Ask the participants what they think about the IEP meeting. Guiding questions may include:

1. What were the legal issues that arose during the meeting?
2. Does the parent have the right to appeal the decision not to use ABA?
3. Does the school need to provide ABA if the program meets Fred's needs?

The answers to these questions will be clarified within the discussion below.

Rationale

5 Minutes

There are more than six million students with disabilities in U.S. public schools. Lawsuits involving students with disabilities against school districts have been on the rise. With a greater understanding of the law, teachers will be able to avoid unnecessary lawsuits and better provide for their students.

Objectives

Post and/or state the following objectives for the lesson plan:

1. Teachers will be able to identify the key distinctions between IDEA, Section 504, and the ADA.
2. Teachers will be able to apply the laws to real-life classroom scenarios.
3. Teachers will be able to better confront special education issues arising in the classroom.

The Law

15 Minutes

After reading the introductory background information below, the principal will divide teachers into four separate groups. Each group will be given markers and pieces of large butcher paper that sticks to the wall. (If there are multiple groups on each topic, the principal may want to ask each group to share one important point to avoid redundancy. The principal will then go around to each group asking for only one point at a time.)

- Group one will cover the Individuals with Disabilities Education Act IDEA (not including discipline),
- Group two will cover disciplining students with disabilities,
- Group three will cover Section 504 of the Rehabilitation Act, and
- Group four will cover the Americans with Disabilities Act (ADA).

Each group will be provided with a content handout. On the butcher paper, the teachers will highlight the most important aspects of the laws. This part of the activity should take between 7 and 10 minutes. Next, the teachers will present this information to the entire group, explaining and reviewing the key aspects of the law.

After each group has the opportunity to create a set of notes on the butcher paper, distribute a note sheet provided below. (*Note*: Also consider asking one person to take notes for the entire group. These notes can be distributed at a later time.)

What happens after 21 if they still need services?

Handout 3.1 Group 1: Individuals with Disabilities Education Act

Identifying Students with Disabilities

States have the duty to identify children ages 0–21 who are in need of services. This duty is known as "child find." A parent, a state education agency, or a local education agency may request an evaluation of a child who is suspected of having a disability. School personnel must obtain parental permission before conducting an evaluation. If a parent refuses to give consent (or refuses to respond to district requests), school officials may begin due process procedures or mediation (discussed below) in order to proceed with the evaluation. It is important to note that it is permissible for school officials to choose not to pursue due process

(*continued*)

Handout 3.1   (continued)

measures or go to mediation if the parents refuse the evaluation. It should also be highlighted that after an evaluation is completed, and the parents do not provide informed consent for services, school officials cannot pursue due process measures or go to mediation in order to obtain consent. And, school officials will not violate the law by not providing services to the child.

The evaluations must be accurate in order to ensure the proper placement of the child. To this end, a variety of assessment tools and strategies should be used (e.g., classroom observation and several different types of tests). If the parents disagree with the evaluation, they may seek an independent evaluation. If the parents opt for an independent evaluation, the school district does not need to accept the results, but they must be considered.

Providing for Students with Disabilities

Each state must provide a student receiving services under IDEA with a free appropriate public education (FAPE). The definition of appropriate has been at issue in several court cases. FAPE does not need to *maximize* a student's learning potential; instead, a FAPE must merely provide a "basic floor of opportunity" for the student. All students receiving services under IDEA are entitled to FAPE.

Why?

The individualized education program (IEP) outlines how a student will receive FAPE. Specifically, based on the student's evaluation, an IEP team prepares the IEP document. The IEP is designed to meet the unique needs of the child and outlines the goals and objectives for the child. The IEP team includes the parents, one general education teacher, one district administrator, one special education teacher, others with expertise that are relevant to the student's needs, and in some cases the student. Students typically participate when they are able to understand and participate in the discussion. School officials must ensure parental participation in the IEP process. Part of this responsibility includes providing parents with notice of their rights under IDEA. Legal controversies have emerged when parents believe that the IEP does not provide their child with a FAPE (see *P.L. v. New York Department of Education*, 2014). Courts will continue to address what level of educational benefit a child must receive under the IDEA (see *Endrew F. v. Douglas Cnty. Sch. Dist.*, 2015).

Students with disabilities must be educated in the **least restrictive environment**—in other words, with students who are not disabled to the maximum extent appropriate. Students with disabilities may only be removed from an educational setting with their general education peers when the instruction in the general education courses cannot be achieved satisfactorily. Factors that are considered in determining the least restrictive environment include: the educational benefits of placing children with disabilities in the general education classroom, the nonacademic benefits of such placements, the effect that the presence of students with disabilities would have on others in the classroom, and the costs associated with the placement. Often parents initiate lawsuits when they believe that their child was not placed in the least restrictive environment (see *B.E.L. v. Hawaii*, 2014).

School districts must also provide related services so that a child with a disability can benefit from special education services. For example, a school district should provide busing services to a student if this service is necessary to deliver special education. Courts have found, however, that medical services are not considered related services (although nursing services, occupational therapy, and physical therapy are considered related services).

Students with disabilities may be required to pass competency exams with accommodations before receiving a high school diploma. Accommodations might include questions in Braille, enlarged answer sheets, additional time, having tests read to students, or sign language

What is due process?; rights State respects due to citizens. balances power protects indies

responses. Before taking a competency exam, students should be given appropriate notice about the exam and the opportunity to learn the academic content. IDEA also requires that school officials provide transition services for students with disabilities (beginning at age 14) who are shifting from school to independent living, work, or postsecondary education. The transition plan should be individualized to meet each student's needs.

Another provision under IDEA is due process for parents, which ensures fairness of educational decisions. Due process occurs when a parent expresses complaints regarding the child's evaluation, identification, or placement. Some of the related procedural safeguards for parents include the following: (1) notification in writing of the referral; (2) ability to grant or deny permission to evaluate the student; (3) notification of IEP meetings (and the right to be present); (4) participation in all decision-making regarding the child with the exception of informal conversations between school officials; (5) bringing an advocate to meetings; and (6) the right to review all of the child's records. If there is a disagreement between the parents and school officials, either side may initiate a due process hearing. It is important to note that IDEA requires that mediation be available to all parties before a due process hearing is conducted. During the mediation session a neutral third party assists parents and school officials to develop a solution. If the issue is not settled in mediation, parents can initiate a due process hearing. Such a hearing involves an independent hearing officer who ultimately makes a decision based upon the evidence presented. If either party is dissatisfied, a complaint can be filed in court.

Handout 3.2 Group 2: Disciplining Students with Disabilities

Disciplining students with disabilities often raises a lot of questions for teachers. Basically, students with disabilities are disciplined in the same manner as students without disabilities, if there is no connection between their misconduct and the disability. However, if a student with a disability is suspended for ten or more total, cumulative days during the school year, the IEP team and other relevant parties must conduct a manifestation determination to decide whether the student's disability is related to the misconduct. If a relationship exists, the IEP team needs to conduct functional behavioral assessments (FBA) and incorporate behavior intervention plans (BIP) into the IEP if necessary. When conducting an FBA, the IEP team develops educational programming that is related to supporting the student's behavioral problems. The team creates a BIP based on the FBA. The BIP should implement several strategies that would prevent the behavior at issue from reoccurring. It is also important to note that when a student who is receiving services under IDEA is removed for more than ten days, it is generally considered a change in placement and requires that the child receives a new IEP. During the time that the new IEP is created, the student needs to remain in their original placement. This is known as the stay put provision.

If the student brings a weapon to school, possesses illegal drugs at school, or inflicts serious bodily harm on another person at school, school officials may forego a manifestation determination and remove a student with a disability to an interim alternative educational setting (IAES) for up to 45 school days. In these cases, a student may be placed unilaterally in an IAES, without the consent of a parent. During these 45 days, FAPE must be provided. Specifically, the child must continue to participate in the curriculum but in another setting. *Yes! makes sense*

Students who have not yet been identified as needing services under IDEA might also get legal protection when removed from the classroom for more than ten days. Specifically, if school officials knew or should have known that a student had a disability before the incident occurred,

(continued)

Handout 3.2   (continued)

the student should not be removed until an IEP team determines the student's eligibility for special education services.

Recent news reports have highlighted discipline issues related to the use of restraint and seclusion in schools. As a result, in 2012, the U.S. Department of Education issued a "Resource Document" to assist school officials with this issue. Despite this guidance, litigation involving restraint and seclusion continues (see, e.g., *Muskrat v. Deer Creek Pub. Sch.*, 2013). One article discusses a recent lawsuit involving a student who was placed in an "isolation box" that was the size of a phone booth to calm her down. Her parents argued that school officials were aware of the child's past trauma involving confinement (see Bouboushan, 2014). The litigation suggests that students' claims related to seclusion and restraint have generally been rejected by courts if school officials' conduct was considered reasonable, not conscience-shocking, and did not cause "obviously excessive" injury to the student (see Eckes & Watts, 2014).

Handout 3.3 Group 3: Section 504 of the Rehabilitation Act and Americans with Disabilities Act

Unlike IDEA, Section 504 is a civil rights law that prohibits those institutions receiving federal funds from discriminating against people with disabilities. Section 504 is a much broader law than IDEA and therefore protects more students. Students who are identified under IDEA also receive protections under Section 504. However, those students receiving services under Section 504 do not automatically receive services under IDEA (e.g., a student in a wheelchair may qualify under Section 504 but not IDEA).

To qualify for services under Section 504, the individual must be a person who has a physical or mental impairment which substantially limits one or more major life activity, has a record of such impairment, and is regarded as having such impairment. A major life activity may include, but is not limited to, seeing, hearing, walking, and talking. Individuals who qualify for services under Section 504 are entitled to reasonable accommodations to facilitate their participation in educational activities. Courts have found that an otherwise qualified individual, under Section 504, is someone who can meet all education or job requirements with reasonable accommodations. A reasonable accommodation might be Braille, a notetaker, a sign language interpreter, or more time on an assignment. On the other hand, a school would not be forced to allow a student who is legally blind to try out for the varsity basketball team—this would be an example of an unreasonable accommodation.

Similar to IDEA, students receiving services under Section 504 must be provided a free appropriate public education and must be educated in the least restrictive environment. When determining FAPE, Section 504 compares the services and treatment provided to students with disabilities to those provided to students without disabilities. The individualized accommodation plan for Section 504 students is called a 504 accommodation plan. Although a written accommodation plan is not required by the law, most school districts do require such a plan.

Similar to Section 504, the ADA was designed to eliminate discrimination based on disability. In 2008, Congress clarified the definition of disability when it passed the ADA Amendments Act. The purpose of the amended legislation was to make it easier to prove an impairment qualified as a disability. Specifically, this law protects those individuals who have a physical or mental impairment that substantially limits one or more major life activities; have a record of impairment; or are regarded as having such an impairment. The ADA incorporates all of the Section 504 law and expands its reach to include all entities—public or private. Both Section 504 and ADA apply to persons of all ages. Those students who are "otherwise qualified" must be permitted to participate in an educational program unless their participation poses a significant safety risk or an undue burden for the school district. Although the ADA is very similar to Section 504 for students, there is one major difference: the ADA requires that school districts **provide access** to individuals with disabilities who are attending school events. Thus, the ADA requires that athletic stadiums, lecture halls, and other facilities be barrier free (e.g., the school should ensure facilities have wheelchair ramps). When removing structural barriers from existing facilities, it must be "readily achievable" and not unduly expensive. When making new structures, however, the building must comply with ADA regulations and be barrier free.

Unlike the IDEA, both Section 504 and the ADA also apply to school district employees. Both laws require school districts to make reasonable accommodations for teachers with disabilities. The accommodation must be reasonable unless it would impose an undue hardship on the employer. "Reasonable" has been interpreted to mean that the accommodation must enable the employee to perform the "essential functions" of the job. Courts often decide what might be a reasonable accommodation. For example, one court ruled that the ADA does not require a district to create a full-time position for a teacher with pedophobia (*Waltherr-Willard v. Mariemont City Schools*, 2015).

Handout 3.4 What's Important to Know About

1. Individuals with Disabilities Education Act IDEA
2. Disciplining Students with Disabilities
3. Section 504 of the Rehabilitation Act and Americans with Disabilities Act (ADA)

Supplemental Activity

Consider sending out the content to this lesson prior to the meeting. Along with the content, provide teachers with one of the three content areas to take notes on. This is one strategy to save time rather than having teachers reading during the professional development session.

Application/Content to Practice

15 Minutes

After the butcher paper presentations are complete, the principal will ask one teacher in each group to act as a moderator as the groups discuss each scenario below. Provide each group with the scenarios. (*Note*: The moderators should be provided with the handout with the scripted guiding questions.)

Handout 3.5   Special Education Scenarios

Scenario One

Parents of an elementary school student with autism requested that the school district provide their child with the Applied Behavior Analysis (ABA) method. The ABA method attempts to ensure a match between the behavioral intervention and the specific behavioral problems at issue. The ABA method is a comprehensive intervention to behavioral issues—it is ideally carried out in every setting possible.

The parents argued that their child would educationally benefit from the ABA method, and in making this argument the parents cited several studies which demonstrated the effectiveness of the ABA. The school district denied this request, arguing that it was too costly and that other methods were equally as effective.

QUESTIONS

1. Would the school district be denying this student FAPE if it did not implement the ABA method? *No b/c basic floor of opportunity*
2. What if the parents pulled their child out of this school and sent him/her to a private school that used the ABA method? Would the parents be able to be reimbursed for the private-school tuition?
3. How would the parents appeal the school district's decision under IDEA?

Scenario Two

A student receiving services under IDEA spray painted graffiti inside the school's restroom. The student painted "Death to Principal Stuckey." The student had already been suspended nine days this academic year. Thus, school officials needed to conduct a manifestation determination before suspending this student for five additional days. The parents argued that their child's diagnosis of attention-deficit hyperactivity disorder (ADHD) was related to his misconduct; thus, he could not be suspended. (*Note:* Although ADHD is not listed as one of the 13 specific categories of disability, it is sometimes included under the "other health impairment" category.)

QUESTIONS

1. Do you think a diagnosis of ADHD could be found to be related to the conduct described above? *IDK, maybe*
2. Do you think that school officials could have moved this student to an interim alternative educational setting for 45 days because of the "death threat" to Principal Stuckey? *Yes*
3. Would a manifestation determination need to be conducted before placing this child in an interim alternative education setting? How would this be decided? *Severity of action?*

Scenario Three

A kindergarten student was diagnosed with acquired immunodeficiency syndrome (AIDS) from a contaminated blood transfusion received at birth. The child's doctors wrote the school district indicating that there was no medical reason why the child should not be able to attend kindergarten. The school district allowed the child to attend. After the child bit another classmate (no skin was broken), school officials had the child evaluated and decided that he should be tutored at home. The child's parents filed a lawsuit, contending that their son should be placed in the kindergarten classroom.

QUESTIONS

1. Would this child be found to be a "handicapped" person under Section 504? Is this student "otherwise qualified" to attend public school? *Wow! Great question. No?*
2. How do school officials balance the rights of the individual student and the safety of the rest of the students in the class?

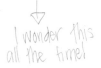

I wonder this all the time!

Scenario Four

School officials dismissed a fifth-grade teacher who suffered epileptic seizures. The school district found out about the seizures because parents had seen the teacher have an episode at the mall and voiced concerns about student safety to the superintendent. After an investigation, school officials learned that even when the teacher took her medication, there was still a very small chance that she could have a seizure. The teacher suffered from approximately two seizures per year. The school board did not renew the teacher's contract. The teacher filed a lawsuit contending that the school board violated her rights under the Americans with Disabilities Act.

QUESTIONS

1. Is this teacher otherwise qualified?
2. What would this teacher argue under Section 504?

Handout 3.6   Special Education Scenarios for Moderators

Scenario One

Question 1: It depends on the facts of the case. The school must provide an educational program that is considered "appropriate." An appropriate education is not necessarily the "best" education. Therefore, if the school's alternative is appropriate, then rejecting the parents' option does not deny FAPE. However, cost is never a justification to deny appropriate services. Further, even if what the parents are suggesting is better than the "floor of opportunity," school officials may want to provide the better services. In the long run, compromise is often less costly than due process and fosters a cooperative relationship. The IEP team would determine whether the ABA method provided the student with a FAPE.

Question 2: The parents would need to demonstrate that the child's placement in the public school was inappropriate and that the private school is appropriate (see *School Committee of Burlington v. Department of Education of Massachusetts*, 1985). Parents who unilaterally place their child in a private school are certainly taking a financial risk. If the public school placement was found to be appropriate, the parents would not be reimbursed. In a recent case, the Third Circuit did not find that the parents were entitled to any reimbursement for private school tuition (see *H.L. v. Downington Area Sch. Dist.*, 2016).

Question 3: The parents must exhaust their administrative options under the IDEA first. Thus, the parents would first participate in a mediation and may eventually participate in a due process hearing with an independent hearing officer.

Scenario Two

Question 1: We obviously need more facts about the student in this scenario, but this issue has certainly arisen in public schools before (see *Richland School District v. Thomas P.*, 2000). Based on the limited facts, however, it could be argued that the student's disability (ADHD) is related to the student's conduct (spray painting). Of course, it could be easily argued that there is no relation between the conduct and the disability. The IEP team would resolve this issue by analyzing the student's prior history and current diagnosis to determine if any relation exists.

Question 2: No. The student could only be unilaterally placed in an interim alternative educational setting for 45 days if the student inflicted serious bodily harm. The student could also be moved to an interim alternative educational setting if the parents agreed. Decisions about the interim alternative educational setting are made by the IEP team, although it may be ordered by a due process hearing officer as well.

Question 3: In this case the graffiti would not meet the three factors to justify an interim alternative educational setting (IAES) without a manifestation determination. However, the 45-day IAES may be used even when the conduct may be related to a student's disability. Thus, no manifestation determination is needed before placing the student in the interim alternative educational setting if drugs, weapons, or an assault was involved.

Scenario Three

Question 1: At least one court has found that the student was a "handicapped person" under Section 504 and was "otherwise qualified" to attend kindergarten in a public school setting after having been diagnosed with AIDS. The court reasoned that there was no significant evidence that the child posed any significant risk of harm to his classmates.

Question 2: In balancing this student's rights under Section 504 and the safety of his classmates, the court noted that there is no medical evidence that AIDS can be spread through biting (see *Thomas v. Atascadero Unified School District*, 1987; *District 27 Community School Board v. Board of Education of the City of New York*, 1986). It should also be noted that when AIDS is reported to public health departments, it must be done in a way that respects the privacy of the student (in the same manner that other diseases are treated with regard to privacy).

Scenario Four

Question 1: This teacher could reasonably argue that she was otherwise qualified under the ADA. In so doing, she may demonstrate that school officials could reasonably accommodate her by training several school officials about how to respond if a seizure were to occur in the classroom. For example, the school nurse or a teacher's aide could be trained in working with the teacher if a seizure occurred in the future.

Question 2: This teacher could also rely upon Section 504, arguing that although she has a physical impairment that substantially limits a major life activity, she is otherwise qualified to teach with reasonable accommodations. She would also contend that she has the necessary physical qualifications for the job.

Assessment

10 Minutes

The principal will assess the participants using a strategy called "Stars and Wishes." The principal will hand out 3 × 5 cards and ask teachers to write three things learned on one side and three things they want to know more about on the other. After a few minutes participants should be asked to share some of their responses to both questions. Principals need to consider what they do with the "wishes" list. For example, principals can provide a summary of the "wishes" to the district's special education director and request that the director respond.

FAQ

10 Minutes

As time permits, you may add some of these additional questions to the followup discussion.

1. **Are the suspension days for students receiving services under IDEA counted cumulatively or consecutively?** not in a row... altogether

   The regulations suggest that 10 cumulative days would be considered a change of placement. It is also important to note that after 10 cumulative days of suspension, educational services would need to be provided to the child. Also, when there is a request for a hearing, the stayput provision applies and the child will remain in his or her present educational placement unless school officials and parents agree on the child's placement.

2. **Must educational services be provided to students receiving services under IDEA if the suspension is 10 days or less?**

   No. When suspensions are less than 10 days, students are treated the same as general education students. If the suspension is more than 10 days, educational services that align with the child's IEP must be provided in the alternative setting.

3. **When must the IEP team convene to develop a behavioral intervention plan, if one has not already been completed?**

   Within 10 business days of any suspension that exceeds 10 cumulative days throughout the school year.

4. **Must school officials administer prescription medication to a student?**

   Yes. School officials must provide related services. This related service of administering medication is more akin to a service provided by a nurse rather than a doctor. Thus, school officials are required to administer medication to students.

5. **Could school officials require students with disabilities to take high-stakes tests?**

   Yes. If the student has been given adequate notice, appropriate curriculum, and necessary accommodations, a test may be administered. The student's IEP must describe the modifications to be made to enable students to participate in the testing. In several states, students with disabilities who do not pass the high-stakes testing requirements are still granted certificates of completion. Certain students with cognitive disabilities may have the option to a take a different test that is based on the same or different achievement standards (e.g., life skills).

6. **What if the costs associated with the child's placement are considered too expensive by the school district?**

   The school must provide the most appropriate placement for the child without regard to the cost. However, it is important to note that appropriate does not mean that school officials are required to maximize a student's potential.

7. **If a parent requests year round schooling for a student receiving services under IDEA, must the school district provide it?**

   Summer school services need only be provided if it is demonstrated that it provides the student with a FAPE. For example, if no services during the summer led to substantial regression, the school district must provide services.

8. **What law would teachers with disabilities rely upon?**

   Section 504 and the ADA would provide protections. In addition, states may have adopted laws providing protections for employees as well. For example, a high school teacher with a mobility impairment in one arm or leg should be employed if a reasonable accommodation can be made to enable performance of essential functions.

9. **Are there state laws that impact students with disabilities?**

   Yes. States have enacted laws that oftentimes mirror and expand upon the requirements of IDEA.

10. **Can you expel a special education student?**

    Yes. If the student's conduct is not related to his or her disability, the student can be expelled. However, during the expulsion, the student must receive educational services as provided by the IEP until age 21. Thus, special education students cannot be expelled in the same manner as nonspecial education students (because the school district must continue educational services to the special education student).

11. **Can parents request that their children be removed from special education programs?**

    Yes. Parents can revoke consent for placement and remove their children out of special education at any time. The parent must revoke services in writing and school districts will not be considered in violation of the law for failing to make FAPE available. Mediation or due process procedures may not be used by school officials to obtain agreement to keep the child in the special education program.

    [handwritten note in margin: What if this impacts other students? negatively?]

12. **Must charter schools accept students with disabilities?**

    Yes. Charter schools must follow federal and state laws. As such, charter schools may not exclude students with disabilities.

13. **Who is really responsible for implementing the IEP?**

    Everyone on the IEP team. However, the classroom teachers must ensure that it is implemented on a daily basis.

14. **Must students with disabilities be accommodated in extracurricular athletics?**

    IDEA's regulations state that school personnel must consider whether an extracurricular or nonacademic activity should be included in the student's IEP. Likewise, Section 504 requires that students with disabilities be provided equal opportunities to participate in physical education courses and extracurricular athletics. The ADA does not permit schools to discriminate on the basis of disability in providing their services, programs, and activities. In 2013, the Office for Civil Rights issued a "Dear Colleague Letter" on the matter providing further guidance. The letter states that school officials should ensure that students with disabilities have consistent opportunities to participate in extracurricular athletics that are equal to those of other students.

15. **Have students with disabilities who have argued a denial of FAPE when they have been severely harassed brought a viable legal claim?**

    The U.S. Department of Education's Office for Civil Rights (OCR) has issued guidance to public schools nationwide in the form of a "Dear Colleague Letter" (Guidance) that focuses on the bullying and harassment of students with disabilities. The Guidance details school officials' responsibilities under Section 504 of the Rehabilitation Act (Section 504) and Title II of the Americans with Disabilities Act (ADA) regarding the bullying of students with disabilities. It adds, "If a student with a disability is being bullied, federal law requires schools to take immediate and appropriate action to investigate the issue and, as necessary, take steps to stop the bullying and prevent it from recurring" (see U.S. Department of Education, 2013b).

Resources/Materials

Relevant Quotes

[W]e know that education is the key to our children's future, and it is the IDEA that ensures all children with disabilities have access to a free appropriate public education. We have seen tremendous progress over the past 25 years—students with disabilities are graduating from high school, completing college, and entering the competitive workforce in record numbers—and we must continue this progress over the next 25 years and beyond.

—President Bill Clinton (2000, in Katsiyannis, Yell, & Bradley, 2001, p. 324)

Free appropriate public education ... evinces a congressional intent to bring previously excluded handicapped children into the public education systems of the states and to require the states to adopt procedures which would result in individualized consideration of and instruction for each child.

—*Board of Education v. Rowley* (1982)

A basic floor of opportunity provided by the Act [IDEA] consists of access to specialized instruction and related services which are individually designed to provide educational benefit to the handicapped child.

—*Board of Education v. Rowley* (1982)

REFERENCES

B.E.L. v. Hawaii, 63 F.Supp.3d 1215 (D. Hawaii, 2014).

Board of Education of the Hendrick Hudson Central School District, v. *Rowley*, 458 U.S. 176 (1982).

Bouboushian, J. (2014, Aug. 5). Parents sue school for its isolation box. *Courthouse News Service*. Retrieved from http://www.courthousenews.com/2014/08/05/70105.htm

District 27 Community School Board v. Board of Education of the City of New York, 502 N.Y.S.2d 325 (N.Y. 1986).

Endrew F. v. Douglas Cnty. Sch. Dist. Re-1, 798 F.3d 1329 (10th Cir. 2015).

Katsiyannis, A., Yell, M., & Bradley, R. (2001). Reflections on the 25th anniversary of the Individuals with Disabilities Education Act. *Remedial and Special Education*, 22, 324–334.

H.L. v. Downington Area Sch. Dist., 624 Fed. Appx 64 (3d Cir. 2016).

Muskrat v. Deer Creek Public School, 715 F.3d 775 (10th Cir. 2013).

P.L. v. New York Department of Education, 56 F.Supp.3d 147 (E.D.N.Y. 2014).

Richland School District v. Thomas P., 2000 U.S. Dist. Lexis 15162 (Wis. 2000).

School Committee of Burlington v. Department of Education of Massachusetts, 471 U.S. 359 (1985).

Thomas v. Atascadero Unified School District, 662 F.Supp. 376 (Cal. 1987).

U.S. Department of Education (2012, May). *Restraint and seclusion: Resource document.* Retrieved from http://www2.ed.gov/policy/seclusion/restraints-and-seclusion-resources.pdf

U.S. Department of Education Office for Civil Rights (2013a, Jan. 25). *Dear colleague letter (disability and athletics).* Retrieved from http://www2.ed.gov/about/offices/list/ocr/letters/colleague-201301-504.pdf

U.S. Department of Education Office of Special Education and Rehabilitative Services (2013b, Aug. 20). *Dear colleague letter (bullying and harassment).* Retrieved from http://www.ed.gov/policy/speced/guid/idea/memosdcltrs/bullyingdcl-8-20-13.doc

Waltherr-Willard v. Mariemont City Schools, 601 Fed. Appx. 385 (6th Cir. 2015).

ADDITIONAL RESOURCES

Alexander, K., & Alexander, M. D. (2011). *American public school law* (8th ed.). Belmont, CA: Wadsworth (See chapter 10).

Eckes, S., & Watts, L.P. (2014, March). The use of restraint and seclusion. *Principal Leadership*, 8–10.

McCarthy, M., Cambron-McCabe, N., & Eckes, S. (2014). *Public school law.* Boston, MA: Allyn and Bacon/Pearson (See chapter 6).

Schimmel, D., Stellman, L., Conlon, C., & Fischer, L. (2014). *Teachers and the law* (9th ed.). Boston, MA: Allyn and Bacon (See chapter 16).

Russo, C. (2009). *Reutter's the law of public education* (7th ed.). New York: Foundation Press (See chapter 14).

Yell, M. (2006). *The law and special education.* Upper Saddle River, NJ: Pearson Prentice Hall.

SUPPLIES AND MATERIALS

- Butcher paper and markers
- 3 × 5 cards

Chapter Four

Discipline

Student Due Process and Search and Seizure

BACKGROUND

When most people think of due process, they think of courtroom trials portrayed on television—of lawyers, judges, juries, witnesses, and dramatic cross-examinations. When people think of search and seizure, they may think of the Fourth Amendment—of warrants, probable cause, and motions to suppress evidence that was seized illegally. The key question addressed in this lesson is: Do these constitutional protections apply to students in the public schools? Specifically,

- Are students entitled to due process? If so, when and what process is due?
- Does the Fourth Amendment protect students against unreasonable search and seizure?

Before the Supreme Court ruled on these questions, many educators feared that if the Bill of Rights applied to students, schools would become courtrooms and education would become an adversarial process. These fears, however, have proven to be greatly exaggerated. This is because the Court has applied the Constitution very differently to students in the public schools than to adults in their homes. This chapter will explain and clarify these differences.

Activator

Motivator

The principal should read each of the scenarios below one at a time. Ask teachers to respond to the set of questions after each scenario.

5 Minutes

Scenario 1: Due Process

Al Anger walked into Principal Pal's office with a note from his teacher stating that Al had started a fight in his classroom for the second time this month. Mr. Pal told Al that because of his fighting, he might be suspended. But before he did so, Pal asked Al if he had anything to say for himself. Al spent 10 minutes explaining that he didn't start the fight and that he was entitled to a due process hearing that included an opportunity for his parents to question his teacher, to have some of his classmates testify on his behalf, and to have his family lawyer advise him. The principal told Al that he believed the teacher, that Al just had his hearing, and that he was being suspended for three days.

Ask teachers, by a show of hands, what they think about each of the statements below. You may want to tally the responses for the group. Ask teachers to hang on to the handout, as they will be returning to it later.

Handout 4.1   Due Process Scenario 1

Al's Issue			
1. Al has the right to some type of due process hearing before being suspended for one to three days.	True	False	Unsure
2. Al has the right to bring a parent to a meeting with the principal before being suspended for more than one day.	True	False	Unsure
3. Before being suspended for ten days, Al has a constitutional right to bring a lawyer to a hearing to advise him.	True	False	Unsure
4. Before suspending Al for one to ten days, the principal must investigate Al's claim by talking with the teacher and/or some of the students.	True	False	Unsure
5. Before expelling Al, he has the right to a formal hearing that includes a written statement of the evidence against him, the right to bring witnesses on his behalf and to question witnesses against him, plus the right to record the hearing and to appeal.	True	False	Unsure
6. If Al were a special education student, he would have additional due process rights.	True	False	Unsure

Scenario 2: Search and Seizure

Read each of the cases below and ask teachers to indicate, by a show of hands, whether they agree, disagree, or are unsure about the claims of Bully's lawyer in cases 1 and 2, the claims of the parents in cases 3 and 4, and the principal's claim in case 5. Tally the responses in each column.

Handout 4.2   Due Process Scenario 2

Case			
1. A student at Yourtown High told Mr. Kalm, the eighth-grade teacher, that she saw Bully Barnes put a long knife in his backpack. Kalm asks Bully if he can look in his backpack for a knife. Bully says, "Sure, 'cause I don't have a knife." Kalm looks through the backpack and can't find a knife. But Kalm opens Bully's wallet and finds an envelope with a substance that he gives to the principal that turns out to be marijuana. The principal then turns the marijuana over to the police. At Bully's trial, his lawyer claims that the search of his backpack was illegal, and therefore the marijuana can't be used as evidence against him.	Agree	Disagree	Unsure
2. Suppose Mr. Kalm had been told that Bully had marijuana in an envelope in his backpack, and when Kalm searched Bully's backpack for the marijuana, he couldn't find any, but he did find a long knife. When a prosecutor introduces the knife as evidence in court, Bully's lawyer claims that the knife was seized illegally since there was no reason to believe Bully had a knife in his backpack.	Agree	Disagree	Unsure
3. When a student tells Principal Kal Koncern that Sharon Shy gave her a pain pill in violation of school rules, Kal tells the nurse to search Sharon. Finding no pills in Sharon's backpack or outer clothing, the nurse continues the search by telling Sharon to take off her clothes and pull out her bra and panties. After no pills are found, Sharon's mother claims that the search violated Sharon's Fourth Amendment rights.	Agree	Disagree	Unsure
5. When teacher Cee Sharp spotted Sue Sly using her cell phone in class in violation of school rules, Sharp took the cell phone and scrolled through Sly's messages. When the teacher saw a message about buying marijuana, she turned the phone over to the principal, who suspended Sly. The student argued that the search violated her Fourth Amendment rights. The principal claimed that Sly's illegal use of the phone in class raised a reasonable suspicion of other improper activity that justified his search.	Agree	Disagree	Unsure

Supplemental Activity

As an alternative activity, principals can discuss the contents of a YouTube clip about the cell phone searches in a school district. This clip discusses how school officials permitted suspicion-less searches of students' cell phones. Show the following clip to the participants: http://www.youtube.com/watch?v=LAN2BKoNjU8

After showing the clip the principal should lead the teachers through a three- to five-minute discussion about whether it was okay to allow these searches.

Rationale

5 Minutes

Teachers often worry about what the legal limits are regarding school disciplinary issues within their classrooms. It is important that teachers understand this area of law in order to respond effectively and legally when such issues arise.

Objectives

Post and/or state the following objectives for the lesson plan:

1. Teachers will be able to examine why and how the U.S. Supreme Court and other courts have applied the Due Process Clause to students in the public schools in cases of suspension and expulsion.
2. Teachers will be able to examine why and how the courts have applied the Fourth Amendment to students in public schools.

The Law

20 Minutes

Two big ideas—due process and search and seizure—are the focus of the content below. In this activity you will ask groups of teachers to conduct a vocabulary activity called a Frayer Diagram. Begin by explaining that a Frayer Diagram is a method for understanding difficult terms. The process begins by providing an example of a Frayer Diagram structure.

Divide teachers into eight groups and assign each group with one term with one Frayer Diagram. Also provide teachers with the handouts 4.5 and 4.6 below. After five to seven minutes, ask a representative from each group to report out their diagrams. (You may want to collect the diagram cards and make a copy for teachers and distribute.)

Handout 4.3   Due Process Key Terms

The Law	Examples
Informal Notice and Hearing	
Definition (your own words)	Implications for Teachers
The Law	Examples
Formal Notice and Hearing	
Definition (your own words)	Implications for Teachers
The Law	Examples
Manifestation Determination	
Definition (your own words)	Implications for Teachers

Handout 4.4   Search and Seizure Key Terms

The Law	Examples
Reasonable Suspicion	
Definition (your own words)	Implications for Teachers

The Law	Examples
BOE v. Earls (2002)	
Definition (your own words)	Implications for Teachers
The Law	Examples
New Jersey v. T.L.O. (1985)	
Definition (your own words)	Implications for Teachers
The Law	Examples
Safford Unified School District No. 1 v. Redding (2009)	
Definition (your own words)	Implications for Teachers

Handout 4.5 Due Process Notes for Distribution

Due Process

In *Goss v. Lopez* (1975), the U.S. Supreme Court ruled that students do not "shed their constitutional rights at the schoolhouse gate." Therefore, they are entitled to some form of due process if they are faced with a possible suspension for 1-to-10 days. This is because a suspension of up to ten days is not so minor a punishment that it may be imposed "in complete disregard of the Due Process Clause."

Due process is a flexible concept. It varies according to the possible seriousness of the penalty: the more serious the possible penalty, the more formal the process that is due.

In cases of a short one to ten-day suspension, the process required is an informal notice and hearing. The informal notice may be oral or in writing and consists of telling students what they are accused of doing and what school rule they are charged with breaking. According to the Supreme Court, if they deny the charge, students are entitled to an informal hearing that consists of (1) "an explanation of the evidence the authorities have," and (2) "an opportunity to tell his side of the story" before the disciplinarian decides on what, if any, punishment to impose. The concern of the Court is that there be at least "rudimentary precautions against unfair or mistaken findings of misconduct" and arbitrary suspensions from school. Thus the Court does not turn schools into courtrooms or require formal due process in cases of short-term suspensions. In fact, the informal process required in these cases is the minimum that most good disciplinarians would follow even if there were no court rulings about student suspensions.

In cases of long-term suspension or expulsion, a formal notice and formal hearing is required. Since such serious penalties can have serious consequences on a student's education and employment opportunities, meticulous procedures must be followed. These consist of a written notice that informs students and their parents of the charges, witnesses, and evidence against them and of their procedural protections at the hearing, including the right to question their accusers, to bring witnesses and evidence on their behalf, to have someone represent them, to record the hearing, and to appeal the decision.

Additional procedures are required for students with special needs. Before they can be suspended for more than a total of ten days during the school year, there must be a manifestation determination. This means that an IEP (individual educational program) team meeting must be called to determine whether the misbehavior is a manifestation of the student's disability. If not, the student can be disciplined like any other student. If the team concludes that the misbehavior is a manifestation of the disability, then standard discipline cannot take place, and the team must conduct a functional behavioral assessment and develop a behavior intervention plan to address the behavior and/or modify the existing plan. (For more on disciplining students with special needs, see chapter 3.)

In sum, due process is not a fixed or inflexible concept that requires the same procedures in all discipline cases. Instead, it is a concept based on fairness that requires more formal procedures before more serious penalties are imposed. That is the reason judges require a formal notice and hearing before expelling a student, an informal process before a 1-to-10-day suspension, and no due process before minor punishments such as detention or probation.

Handout 4.6   Search and Seizure Notes for Distribution

Search and Seizure

In *New Jersey v. T.L.O.* (1985), the Supreme Court ruled that the Fourth Amendment's protection against unreasonable search and seizure applies to students in the public schools. However, the Court explained that educators are not required to comply with the requirements that apply to police, who must obtain a warrant from a judge based on probable cause before searching citizens in their homes. Educators do not need a warrant. Instead of probable cause (a relatively high standard of evidence required of police before a judge will issue a warrant), the lower standard required of teachers or administrators is reasonable suspicion. Specifically, to justify a search by educators, the search must be reasonable in its inception and in its scope. To be reasonable in inception, a school official must be able to articulate some objective reason for the search. Furthermore, the scope of the search must be related to its reason and not be excessively intrusive in light of the age and sex of the student and the nature of the infraction. For example, if one student reported that he saw another student put a pistol in his backpack, it would be reasonable in inception to search the backpack. But it would not be reasonable in scope for the educator to open and search the wallet in the backpack since it could not contain a pistol.

In *Board of Education v. Earls* (2002), the Supreme Court held that schools could require students to sign waivers permitting random, suspicion-less drug testing as a condition for participating in *any* extracurricular activity. In a 5–4 decision, the majority reasoned that participation in extracurricular activities is a privilege and not a right. The Court further justified its decision based on the school's responsibility to protect the health and safety of students and on its belief that the goal of a drug-free school outweighed the limited invasion of privacy involved in random urine testing.

In *Safford Unified School District No. 1 v. Redding* (2009), the Supreme Court ruled that information from one student that a classmate gave her a pain pill in violation of school rules constituted reasonable suspicion to justify a search of the student's backpack and outer clothing. But the court also ruled that proceeding to a strip search was not reasonable in scope. This is because the search was for a common pain reliever that posed no danger to the students (the drug was limited in power and quantity), and there was no reason to think the student was carrying pills in her underwear. Thus a search, even if justified at its inception, crosses the constitutional boundary when it becomes excessively intrusive in light of the age and sex of the student, especially when the object of the search poses no danger to students.

Application/Content to Practice

15 Minutes

Ask teachers to revisit the hypothetical cases from the start of this lesson. Individually or in small groups ask teachers to answer the questions regarding due process (in handout 4.7) and search and seizure (in handout 4.8). The answers to each of the scenarios are provided for the principal to share.

Handout 4.7   Due Process Scenarios Revisited

Due process		
Issue	**True/False**	**Why?**
1. Al is entitled to some type of due process hearing before being suspended for one to three days.		
2. Al is entitled to bring a parent to a meeting with the principal before being suspended for more than one day.		
3. Before being suspended for ten days, Al would be entitled to bring a lawyer to a hearing to advise him.		
4. Before suspending Al for one to ten days, the principal must investigate Al's claim by talking with the teacher and/ or some of the students.		
5. Before expelling Al, he has the right to a formal hearing that includes a written statement of the evidence against him, the right to bring witnesses on his behalf and to question witnesses against him, plus the right to record the hearing and to appeal.		
6. If Al were a special education student, he would have additional due process rights.		

Handout 4.8   Search and Seizure Scenarios Revisited

Search and Seizure		
Case	**Agree/ Disagree**	**Why?**
1. A student at Yourtown High told Mr. Kalm, the eighth-grade teacher, that she saw Bully Barnes put a long knife in his backpack. Kalm asks Bully if he can look in his backpack for a knife. Bully says, "Sure, 'cause I don't have a knife." Kalm looks through the backpack and can't find a knife. But Kalm opens Bully's wallet and finds an envelope with a substance that he gives to the principal that turns out to be marijuana. The principal then turns the marijuana over to the police. At Bully's trial, his lawyer claims that the search of his backpack was illegal, and therefore the marijuana can't be used as evidence against him.		
2. Suppose Mr. Kalm had been told that Bully had marijuana in an envelope in his backpack, and when Kalm searched Bully's backpack for the marijuana, he couldn't find any, but he did find a long knife. When a prosecutor introduces the knife as evidence in court, Bully's lawyer claims that the knife was seized illegally since there was no reason to believe Bully had a knife in his backpack.		

Handout 4.8 *(continued)*

Search and Seizure		
3. When a student tells principal Kal Koncern that Sharon Shy gave her a pain pill in violation of school rules, Kal tells the nurse to search Sharon. Finding no pills in Sharon's backpack or outer clothing, the nurse continues the search by telling Sharon to take off her clothes and pull out her bra and panties. After no pills are found, Sharon's mother claims that the search violated Sharon's Fourth Amendment rights.		
4. The Yourtown School Board is concerned about drug use. Therefore, the board wants to require all students who want to participate in any extracurricular activity to sign a waiver agreeing to submit to random, suspicion-less drug testing. Some parents claim that forcing their children to submit to drug testing when there is no reasonable suspicion that they have used drugs is a violation of their Fourth Amendment privacy rights.		
5. When teacher Cee Sharp spotted Sue Sly using her cell phone in class, in clear violation of school rules, Sharp took the phone and scrolled through Sly's messages. When the teacher saw a message about buying marijuana, she gave the phone to the principal, who suspended Sly. The student argued that the search of the phone violated her Fourth Amendment rights. The principal claimed that the improper use of the phone in class raised a reasonable suspicion of illegal activity that justified his search.		

Due Process Answers

1. True.

According to the Supreme Court decision in *Goss*, Al Anger is entitled to an informal hearing before being suspended for one to ten days. This consists of telling Al what rule he is accused of breaking. If he denies the accusation, he is entitled to know the evidence against him and to be given an opportunity to tell his side of the story before the principal decides on what, if any, punishment to impose.

2. False.

Although some schools allow a student to bring a parent to a conference before imposing a suspension if the student is not a danger to himself or others, this is a matter of discretion and is not required by the courts.

3. False.

Al does not have a constitutional right to bring a lawyer to advise him in the informal hearing that is required before a short-term suspension. According to the Supreme Court opinion in *Goss*, "further formalizing the suspension process … may not only make it too costly as a regular disciplinary tool but also destroy its effectiveness as part of the teaching process." However, courts have held that in an expulsion case, Al would have a right to bring a lawyer to attend the hearing and advise him because of the seriousness of the possible penalty.

4. **False**.

The *Goss* decision does not always require the principal to interview teachers or students. In cases of short suspensions, whether and how much to investigate is a matter of administrative judgment, and, in many situations, that would be the right thing to do.

5. **True**.

Before an expulsion, Al would be entitled to a written notice that advised him of the charges and evidence against him and of his right to bring someone to represent him and to bring witnesses and evidence on his behalf as well as his right to question witnesses, and his right to record the hearing and appeal the decision.

6. **True**.

If Al were a special education student, he could not be suspended for more than ten days during a school year unless his IEP team held a manifestation determination that concluded that his misbehavior was not caused by his disability.

Search and Seizure Answers

1. **Bully's lawyer is *right*.**

The search of Bully's wallet and the seizure of his marijuana were illegal. According to the *T.L.O.* decision, the Fourth Amendment requires that a search by educators must be reasonable in inception and scope. Based on what the student informant told Kalm, it was reasonable in inception for him to search the backpack for the long knife. But it was not reasonable in scope to search the wallet since a long knife could not be in the wallet. Therefore, if a prosecutor wanted to introduce the drugs as evidence in a criminal trial, Bully's lawyer would probably be successful in having the evidence ruled inadmissible.

2. **The seizure of the knife was *legal*.**

Based on the student informant's information, Kalm's search of the backpack to look for the drugs was reasonable in inception. Since he found the knife in plain view incidental to a search for drugs, the search was not excessive in scope. Therefore, the judge would allow the knife to be entered in evidence against Bully.

3. **The strip search was *not legal*.**

Applying the principles of *Safford v. Redding* to the facts of this case, the search violated Sharon's Fourth Amendment rights. Although the initial search of Sharon's backpack and outer clothing was reasonable in inception, the search was not reasonable in scope because the pills posed no danger to students, and there was no reason to believe Sharon was hiding them in her underwear.

4. **The drug testing would be *legal*.**

According to the *Earls* decision, public schools have discretion to require students to sign waivers allowing school officials to engage in random, suspicion-less drug testing in order to participate in extracurricular activities. There is much debate about whether such a requirement is wise and cost-effective. But it is now clear that such a policy does not violate the Fourth Amendment.

5. The principal's search was *illegal*.

In 2014, a federal appeals court ruled that simply using a cell phone on school grounds does not give school officials the right to search any content stored in the phone.

The fact that a student sent a text message in violation of school rules justifies the confiscation of the phone. But it does not justify searching the phone if there is no independent reason to believe that the student is engaged in some illegal activity.

Assessment

5 *Minutes*

At the beginning of the lesson two questions were highlighted as the primary purpose of this lesson. Now, in the assessment, return to these two questions. Provide teachers with a ticket to leave the meeting. On one side ask the teachers to answer the question: Are students entitled to due process? If so, when and what process is due? On the other, ask them to respond to the other question: When may educators search students without violating the Fourth Amendment?

Handout 4.9   Assessment Tickets

Due process question	*Search and seizure question*
Are students entitled to due process? If so, when and what process is due?	When may educators search students without violating the Fourth Amendment?

Supplemental Activity

Use the following T/F assessment:

1. Students are entitled to an informal notice and hearing before short suspensions of one to ten days.
2. Before being expelled, students must be provided with a lawyer by the school if they can't afford one.
3. Administrators can strip-search students if they have probable cause to believe the student stole large sums of money.
4. Before expelling students, they are entitled to a formal notice and hearing. The written notice must inform students and their parents of the evidence against them and of their rights at the hearing including the opportunity to have someone represent them, to bring witnesses and evidence on their behalf, to question their accusers, to record the hearing, and to appeal.
5. Students have a right to remain silent when questioned by teachers about violations of school rules.

6. To justify a search of students' clothing, backpacks or cars, teachers or administrators need "reasonable suspicion." To meet this standard, the search must be reasonable in its inception and reasonable in scope.
7. Schools may require students to sign waivers to permit random, suspicion-less drug testing in order to participate in extracurricular activities.

Answers

1. True.
2. False. (In many states, students may bring a lawyer to an expulsion hearing to advise them. But the school is not required to furnish a lawyer for the student.)
3. False. (Strip searches are only permitted in situations that pose a serious danger to the student or others.)
4. True.
5. False. (This only applies to criminal law.)
6. True.
7. True.

FAQ

As time permits, you may add some of these additional questions to the follow-up discussion.

10 Minutes

1. **Do *Miranda* warnings apply to students?**
No. In *Miranda v. Arizona*, 377 U.S. 201 (1966), the Supreme Court ruled that the Fifth Amendment privilege against self-incrimination applies in a criminal investigation and requires that suspects be informed of their right to remain silent, that what they say may be used against them, and that they have a right to have a lawyer represent them.

   These rules do not apply to educators or to school resource officers employed by the school who question students in public schools since school discipline is not a criminal proceeding. However, *Miranda* would apply to police who question students in school as part of a criminal investigation.
2. **Is due process required before in-school suspension?**
Not usually. A federal appeals court ruled that students are not generally entitled to notice and an opportunity to be heard before an in-school suspension. The court reasoned that most in-school suspensions do not deprive students of educational opportunities the way an out-of-school suspension does. In this case, the student was not deprived of education because she was required to complete her academic assignments while serving her in-school suspension. However, the court recognized that under certain circumstances, in-school isolation might constitute as much deprivation of education as at-home suspension, and in that case the student would be entitled to due process protections. *Laney v. Farley*, 501 F.3d 577 (6th Cir. 2007).

3. **Must due process be used before corporal punishment?**

Not in those states or school districts that permit corporal punishment. The Supreme Court has ruled that corporal punishment is not unconstitutional and that it is a matter for state legislatures and local school districts to decide whether to permit such punishment and, if so, what procedures to require. However, courts have ruled that grossly excessive corporal punishment may be unconstitutional, and such punishment probably also violates state law. *Ingraham v. Wright*, 430 U.S. 651 (1977).

4. **Are strip searches unconstitutional?**

Often, but not always. Strip-searching two second-grade students for a missing $7 dollars was ruled clearly unconstitutional. In that case, the court suggested a continuum: at one extreme are dangerous weapons and drugs that might justify a strip search. At the other extreme are small amounts of money, personal items, and "non-dangerous" contraband that would never justify strip searches. *Jenkins by Hall v. Talladega City Bd. of Educ.*, 95 F.3d 1036 (11th Cir. 1996).

Similarly, another court ruled that a strip search for $100 missing from a teacher's purse was unreasonable since the stealing of money involved little danger to others and thus cannot justify a highly invasive search. In cases where school officials feel that students should be strip searched because of substantial evidence of criminal behavior such as possession of dangerous weapons or distribution of illegal drugs, it would be wise to have police—rather than educators—conduct such searches.

5. **What about searches of student lockers or cars?**

Courts differ about whether the Fourth Amendment even applies to lockers. Some judges have ruled that students have no reasonable expectation of privacy in their lockers. This is because the lockers are owned by the school, and school rules usually make it clear that the lockers are subject to search by school officials— especially when they have the combination of the locks. A few courts hold that educators should have some individual suspicion before they search a student's locker—especially if they search jackets or other items owned by the student in the locker. This is based on the theory that students do not lose their reasonable expectation of privacy in their clothing when they put it in their locker.

Courts consider the search of a car on school property more like the search of a backpack than a locker, and the principles of *T.L.O.* should apply. Thus, to comply with the Fourth Amendment, educators' searches of students' cars should be based on individual suspicion and be reasonable in inception and reasonable in scope.

6. **Is it constitutional for administrators to use video cameras for surveillance?**

Usually it is. Video cameras may be used in school hallways, cafeterias, libraries, parking lots and other "common areas" without violating constitutional principles. However, the Fourth Amendment might be violated if video cameras were placed in school bathrooms, locker rooms, or private offices where people have a "reasonable expectation of privacy."

7. **If students consent to a search, do they lose their Fourth Amendment protections?**

Yes, if they consent voluntarily. In a school setting, however, a student's lawyer might raise two questions: Is it reasonable to hold that students waived their rights if they didn't know them? Second, was the student's acquiescence to an administrator's request to search really voluntary? The answers may depend on the age and maturity of the student and whether the situation in which the consent was given seemed voluntary or coercive.

8. **Can educators ask the school resource officer to search a student's backpack?**

   Yes, if the educator has reasonable suspicion that the student has committed a crime or violated a school rule (e.g., a teacher smells marijuana or sees a knife in a student's backpack). SROs are not held to the same Fourth Amendment standards as police.

Resources/Materials

Related Cases

- In an Ohio case, an eighth-grade student agreed to take a drug test after being told that he would be expelled if he refused. Although there was no reasonable suspicion to justify the search, the school argued that the search was justified because the student consented to the test. The judge explained that if consent is voluntary, a court will not question the reasonableness of the search. But here the judge ruled that the search was not voluntary. It was secured by coercion and threat: the student had to waive his Fourth Amendment rights or be expelled (*Cummerlander v. Patriot Prep. Academy*, 2015).

- When school officials received reports that a high school student smoked marijuana on the school bus, they searched the student's pockets, backpack, shoes, and cell phone. A federal appeals court ruled that the search of the student's clothing was reasonable in inception. However, the search of the cell phone was not. According to the judge, "No reasonable school administrator could believe that searching a student's cell phone would result in finding marijuana—the purpose for which the administrator initiated the search" (*Gallimore v. Henrico County School Board*, 2014).

- A Florida court ruled that an anonymous tip naming a specific student about a serious danger constituted reasonable suspicion to justify the search of a book bag and the seizure of a loaded handgun (*K.P. v. State*, 2013).

- Students successfully challenged a school policy that required all students to submit to suspicion-less body pat-down searches before attending their prom or graduation. The judge acknowledged the school's legitimate concern in minimizing drug use and drinking—especially at proms. But the judge ruled that less intrusive methods to detect contraband—such as magneticometric wands or visual inspection—should first be tried to establish individual suspicion before resorting to a body pat-down of all students (*Herrera v. Santa Fe Public Schools*, 2013).

- A federal court wrote that an out-of-district student had no due process right to challenge a school's decision not to admit him. However, the court ruled that once the student was enrolled, he could not be expelled without due process.

Relevant Quotes

The authority possessed by the State to prescribe and enforce standards of conduct in its schools although concededly very broad must be exercised consistently with constitutional safeguards. Among other things, the State is constrained to recognize a student's legitimate entitlement to a public education as a property interest which is protected by the Due Process Clause and which may not be taken away for misconduct without adherence to the minimum procedures required by that clause ...

The concern would be mostly academic if the disciplinary process were a totally accurate, unerring process, never mistaken and never unfair. Unfortunately, that is not the case, and no one suggests that it is ...

Requiring effective notice and informal hearing permitting the student to give his version of the events will provide a meaningful hedge against erroneous action. At least the disciplinarian will be alerted to the existence of disputes about facts and arguments about cause and effect. He may then determine himself to summon the accuser, permit cross-examination, and allow the student to present his own witnesses ... In any event his discretion will be more informed and we think the risk of error substantially reduced ...

We have imposed requirements which are, if anything, less than a fair-minded school principal would impose upon himself in order to avoid unfair suspensions.

—Goss v. Lopez (1975)

How should we strike the balance between the schoolchild's legitimate expectations of privacy and the school's equally legitimate need to maintain an environment in which learning can take place? It is evident that the school setting requires some easing of the restrictions to which searches by public authorities are ordinarily subject. The warrant requirement, in particular, is unsuited to the school environment: requiring a teacher to obtain a warrant before searching a child suspected of an infraction of school rules (or of the criminal law) would unduly interfere with the maintenance of the swift and informal disciplinary procedures needed in the schools ...

The school setting also requires some modification of the level of suspicion of illicit activity needed to justify a search. Ordinarily, a search ... must be based on "probable cause" to believe that a violation of the law has occurred ... [However,] the legality of a search of a student should depend simply on the reasonableness, under all the circumstances, of the search ... Under ordinary circumstances, a search of a student by a teacher or other school official will be justified at its inception when there are reasonable grounds for suspecting that the search will turn up evidence that the student has violated either the law or the rules of the school. Such a search will be permissible in its scope when the measures adopted are reasonably related to the objectives of the search and not excessively intrusive in light of the age and sex of the student and the nature of the infraction.

—New Jersey v. T.L.O. (1985)

Given the nationwide epidemic of drug use, and the evidence of increased drug use in Tecumseh schools, it was entirely reasonable for the School District to enact this particular drug testing policy ... The test results are not turned over to any law enforcement authority ... The only consequence of a failed drug test is to limit the student's privilege of participating in extracurricular activities … Given the minimally intrusive nature of the sample collection and the limited uses to which the test results are put, we conclude that the invasion of students' privacy is not significant …

Within the limits of the Fourth Amendment, local school boards must assess the desirability of drug testing schoolchildren. In upholding the constitutionality of the policy, we express no opinion as to its wisdom. Rather, we hold only that Tecumseh's Policy is a reasonable means of furthering the School District's important interest in preventing and deterring drug use among schoolchildren.

—*Board of Education v. Earls* (2002)

The *T.L.O.* concern to limit a school search to reasonable scope requires the support of reasonable suspicion of danger … before a search can reasonably make the quantum leap from outer clothes and backpacks to exposure of intimate parts. The meaning of such a search, and the degradation its subject may reasonably feel, place a search that intensive in a category of its own.

—*Safford Unified School District No. 1 v. Redding* (2009)

REFERENCES

Board of Education v. Earls, 536 U.S. 822 (2002).
Cummerlander v. Patriot Prep. Academy, 86 F.Supp.3d 808 (2015).
Gallimore v. Henrico County School Board, 38 F.Supp.3d 721 (2014).
G.C. v. Owensboro Public Schools, 711 F.3d 623 (6th Cir. 2013).
Goss v. Lopez, 419 U.S. (1975).
Herrera v. Santa Fe Public Schools, 792 F.Supp.2d 1174 (2013).
Ingraham v. Wright, 430 U.S. 651 (1975).
Jenkins by Hall v. Talladega City Board of Education, 95 F.3d 1036 (11th Cir. 1996).
Klump v. Nazareth Area School District, 425 F.Supp.2d 622 (2006).
K.P. v. State, 129 So.3d 1121 (Fla. Ct. App. 2013).
Laney v. Farley, 501 F.3d 577 (6th Cir. 2007).
Miranda v. Arizona, 377 U.S. 201 (1966).
New Jersey v. T.L.O., 469 U.S. 325 (1985).
Safford Unified School District No.1 v. Redding, 557 U.S. 364 (2009).

ADDITIONAL RESOURCES

Alexander, K., & Alexander, M. D. (2011). *American public school law* (8th ed.). Belmont, CA: Wadsworth (See chapters 8 and 9).
McCarthy, M., Cambron-McCabe, N., & Eckes, S. (2014). *Public school law* (7th ed.). Boston, MA: Allyn and Bacon/Pearson (See chapter 7).
Schimmel, D., Stellman, L., Conlon, C., & Fischer, L. (2015). *Teachers and the law* (9th ed.). Boston, MA: Allyn and Bacon (See chapter 13).
Russo, C. (2009). *Reutter's the law of public education* (7th ed.). New York: Foundation Press (See chapter 13).

Chapter Five

Student Harassment and Bullying

BACKGROUND

Court decisions highlight that school officials have a responsibility to provide a safe educational environment free from bullying and peer sexual harassment. There is no federal law that directly addresses bullying, but all fifty states have enacted laws to prevent bullying in schools. Bullying often overlaps with harassment. In peer sexual harassment lawsuits, school boards may be liable for monetary damages if they were deliberately indifferent to known acts of peer sexual harassment in the schools. These cases generally involve a Title IX claim, which is a federal law that prohibits discrimination based on sex. In some cases, students with disabilities who have been harassed at school are initiating lawsuits under the Americans with Disabilities Act, Section 504 of the Rehabilitation Act, and/or the Individuals with Disabilities in Education Act (IDEA). This lesson plan will focus on how school districts can avoid liability for bullying and harassment while providing a safe and welcoming environment for all students.

Activator

Motivator

7 Minutes

There are several different clips available on YouTube that discuss harassment and bullying. One very helpful clip can be found at https://www.youtube.com/watch?v=c08oEqvbivo.

If you are unable to access the clip, please read the following summary:

A fourteen-year-old student committed suicide after he experienced severe harassment and bullying from his peers—sometimes in the school hallway. The clip does not discuss whether school officials knew about the harassment. For the purposes of this exercise,

please think about whether there could be school district liability had school officials been
aware that other students were bullying him on a daily basis.

Principals will lead a discussion on the video from the YouTube clip. If a YouTube clip
is not used, the questions below would still apply to the summary of the clip provided
above. Some questions that may guide this discussion include:

- When might school officials be liable in a case involving similar facts?
- Would the outcome be different if school officials had knowledge of the harassment?

Rationale

3 Minutes

Studies have indicated that as many as 80 percent of students experience some form of sexual harassment in public schools. These statistics
are troublesome considering that peer sexual harassment and bullying
can have long-term psychological effects on student victims. Indeed,
harassment and bullying are serious problems that may impact some students' academic achievement and social well-being.

Objectives

Post and/or state the following objectives for the lesson plan:

1. Teachers will be able to apply the legal standard to real-life situations that occurred
   in U.S. public schools to determine school board liability for peer harassment.
2. Teachers will be able to avoid school district liability in peer harassment cases that
   occur in their classrooms.
3. Teachers will become familiar with trends in antibullying state legislation.

The Law

20 Minutes

To help teachers understand the laws associated with student harassment and bullying, you will have them engage in a Think, Pair, Share
activity. To begin, ask teachers to partner (pair up). One partner will
get the *Davis* Case Handout and the other the Students with Disabilities
Handout. Next, ask teachers to read their case individually and to *think* about what
the case means in regard to the law. Then ask teachers to *share* the case and what they
learned and implications with their *pair* partner. The principals can bring the large
group back together and ask volunteers to summarize what they learned.

Handout 5.1 *Davis* **Case**

The responsibility of school districts to take action against peer sexual harassment was recognized in a 1999 U.S. Supreme Court decision, *Davis v. Monroe County Board of Education*. The
Court explained in *Davis* that school officials have clear responsibilities to respond to known
acts of peer sexual harassment in public schools. When school officials are deliberately indifferent to the sexual harassment, school districts can be held financially liable.

   Most of the recent peer sexual harassment lawsuits, including the *Davis* decision, have been
based on Title IX of the Education Amendments of 1972, which prohibits sex discrimination

under any education program or activity receiving federal financial assistance. Title IX has been interpreted broadly to cover peer harassment and also covers cases involving teachers harassing students. It is important to note that state laws may also address obligations regarding sex discrimination in schools.

In *Davis*, a fifth-grade female student was allegedly subjected to a prolonged pattern of sexual harassment. According to the complaint, the offending male student attempted to touch LaShonda's breasts and genital area and made vulgar comments toward her. Additionally, in one incident the male student placed a doorstop in his pants and acted in a sexually aggressive manner with the female student. The female student and her mother notified a coach, several teachers, and the principal about the various incidents of harassment throughout the school year. School officials, however, failed to effectively respond to these complaints and only threatened possible action. Based on the female student's dropping grades and a suicide note, her mother contended that the continued harassment and the school's failure to respond affected her daughter's education.

In examining this issue, the Supreme Court established a standard of school district liability for peer sexual harassment under Title IX. In addition to the harassment being based on sex, the following four factors must be present for a school district to be found liable for peer sexual harassment:

1. appropriate school officials must have actual knowledge of the harassment;
2. school officials must have responded with deliberate indifference to the harassment (e.g., they did not do anything to stop the harassment or their response was clearly unreasonable);
3. the harassment must have been severe, pervasive, and objectively offensive; and
4. the harassment must have had a negative impact on a student's education.

When applying these four factors in the *Davis* decision, the Court found the school district to be liable for peer sexual harassment. It is important to note that all four factors must be proven for a school district to be held liable. For example, in this case, a mere drop in grades would have been insufficient to prove that the harassment was actionable. However, in conjunction with the other three factors in this case, the grades provided evidence of a connection between the offender's conduct and the denial of educational benefits. The plaintiff's claim also relied on the severity of the harassment and the school's knowledge of and deliberate indifference to the harassment. It is also important to note that school officials must have control over the harasser and the environment in order to be liable.

Oftentimes in Title IX peer harassment court decisions, the outcome of the case will focus on whether school officials did enough to appropriately respond to the harassment. In a recent case, a male student alleged that he frequently heard inappropriate sexual remarks, was called gay, and experienced another student exposing his genitals, among other offensive acts at the school. School officials responded by rearranging the classroom for the student to avoid the perpetrator as well as suspending the perpetrator on a few occasions (*Doe v. Board of Education of Prince George's County*, 2015). The Fourth Circuit Court of Appeals found that school officials took steps to address the harassment and that their actions were not clearly unreasonable.

Handout 5.2   Harassment and Bullying—Students with Disabilities

There is a growing body of litigation involving the harassment and bullying of students with disabilities (*Long v. Murray*, 2013; *Moore v. Chilton Cnty. Bd. of Educ.*, 2014). In addition to the increasing number of lawsuits, the U.S. Department of Education (USDoE) has stated that it "has received an ever-increasing number of complaints concerning the bullying of students with disabilities" (p. 1). In response, the USDoE has published two recent letters providing schools with guidance about their responsibility to address disability-based harassment. First, in 2013, the USDoE's Office of Special Education and Rehabilitative Services (OSERS) issued a "Dear Colleague Letter" to address bullying and harassment of students with disabilities receiving

(continued)

Handout 5.2   *(continued)*

> services under IDEA (see http://www.ed.gov/policy/speced/guid/idea/memosdcltrs/bullyingdcl-
> 8-20-13.doc). The guidance cites research highlighting that students with disabilities are dispro-
> portionately affected by bullying.
>
>   The second recent letter addressing this issue was issued by the Office for Civil Rights (OCR)
> in 2014 (see http://www2.ed.gov/about/offices/list/ocr/letters/colleague-bullying-201410.pdf).
> In these types of disability-based harassment cases, sometimes a court might apply the *Davis*
> standard or instead might apply a different standard and ask whether school officials acted in
> "bad faith" or engaged in "gross misjudgment" when analyzing disability-based harassment
> claims. The letter explains that bullying a student with a disability on any basis can result in a
> denial of a Free Appropriate Public Education (FAPE).

Application/Content to Practice

15 Minutes

The principal will split the teachers into groups of three to four. Each group will read and discuss all four scenarios. In so doing, the teachers should apply the *Davis* standard to determine whether the school district would be legally liable for harassment based on sex. Ask the participants to circle all the standards that apply to each case.

Handout 5.3   Scenarios and the *Davis* Standard

Scenario	*Davis* Standard
1 Jane, a sixth-grade student, was subjected to severe and continuous harassment. The harassment began when she was referred to as the "German gay girl" (*Vance v. Spencer County Public School District*, 2000). The harassment continued when another student asked the female student to describe oral sex. Jane was also regularly shoved into walls and her homework was destroyed on several occasions. During one particular bathroom break from class, several boys called Jane names such as whore and bitch. While doing so, two of the boys held her hands and the other grabbed her hair and started yanking her shirt off. One of the boys stated that he wanted to have sex with her. School officials responded to several such complaints from Jane and her mother by speaking with the boys, but their response was not effective. Specifically, the boys were only spoken to and not punished. After they were spoken to, Jane contended that the harassment grew worse.	1. Appropriate school officials must have actual knowledge of the harassment. 2. School officials must have responded with deliberate indifference to the harassment (e.g., they did not do anything to stop the harassment or their response was clearly unreasonable). 3. The harasser's behavior must have been severe, pervasive, and objectively offensive. 4. The harassment must have had a negative impact on a student's education.

Scenario	Davis Standard
When the harassment continued throughout the following school year, Jane and her mother filed a complaint, pursuant to the school harassment policy. The school claimed that it did not have enough information to investigate. Jane was later diagnosed with depression and withdrew from school. She and her mother then filed a lawsuit against the district. Would the school district be held liable in this situation?	
2 Mary, a high school student, was sexually assaulted by two male students (*Doe v. East Haven Board of Education*, 2006). It took her about three months to report the assault to school officials. After Mary told school officials that she had been sexually assaulted, the boys called her a "slut, a liar, a bitch, a whore," and other students began to taunt her. Mary and her mother lodged repeated complaints with the superintendent, the principal, and the guidance counselor; the parent felt that the complaints were ignored. Several weeks after receiving the complaints, the school district responded. The school officials argued that they provided the female student with a separate room in the guidance office where she could go if she felt uncomfortable. In the meantime, Mary became withdrawn, missed some school, and had suicidal thoughts. Would the school district be held liable in this situation?	1. Appropriate school officials must have actual knowledge of the harassment. 2. School officials must have responded with deliberate indifference to the harassment (e.g., they did not do anything to stop the harassment or their response was clearly unreasonable). 3. The harasser's behavior must have been severe, pervasive, and objectively offensive. 4. The harassment must have had a negative impact on a student's education.
3 Tom and Sally were high school juniors and classmates. Tom repeatedly asked Sally for a date and she repeatedly refused. After the third request, Sally complained to her teacher, who told Tom to stop bothering Sally. The following week Tom asked again and tried to kiss Sally. As a result, her mother complained to the principal and asked him to move Tom to another class. Instead, the principal called Tom to his office, ordered him to stop harassing Sally, and warned of consequences if he did not. The following week, Tom kissed Sally, who became extremely upset. As a result, she was enrolled in a private school and sued the school district for failing to prevent the harassment. Should the school be held liable?	1. Appropriate school officials must have actual knowledge of the harassment. 2. School officials must have responded with deliberate indifference to the harassment (e.g., they did not do anything to stop the harassment or their response was clearly unreasonable). 3. The harasser's behavior must have been severe, pervasive, and objectively offensive. 4. The harassment must have had a negative impact on a student's education.

Handout 5.3   (*continued*)

Scenario	*Davis* Standard
4 A student with a disability receiving services under Section 504 and the IDEA experienced harassment and bullying in the classroom on a daily basis throughout her fourth-grade year. A few students in the class frequently referred to her as "retard" and would often knock her books out of her hands when she was in the hallway. During recess, kids would try to trip her and teased her about her thick glasses and stutter. The student's mother complained to the teacher, who did speak with the perpetrators' parents on several occasions. When the harassment continued, the mother reached out to both the principal and the superintendent. They held meetings with the student's teacher to develop ways to keep her safe. Unfortunately, the harassment continued, and on one occasion she was punched in the bathroom. As a result, the mother sued the school district under Title IX and Section 504. Should the school be liable?	1. Appropriate school officials must have actual knowledge of the harassment. 2. School officials must have responded with deliberate indifference to the harassment (e.g., they did not do anything to stop the harassment or their response was clearly unreasonable). 3. The harasser's behavior must have been severe, pervasive, and objectively offensive. 4. The harassment must have had a negative impact on a student's education. With regard to the disability harassment claim, did school officials act in "bad faith" or engage in "gross misjudgment"?

Principals should use the following outcomes for each case to drive the discussion. These key points can also be used as a handout or a presentation slide.

Handout 5.4   Case Scenario Outcomes

Scenario	Outcome
1	The court ruled in favor of Jane, finding that the sexual harassment was so severe, pervasive, and objectively offensive that it deprived her of access to the educational opportunities provided by the school and that school officials had actual knowledge of the harassment and were deliberately indifferent to the harassment. Because of the numerous complaints to several different school officials, the actual notice factor was clearly met. A jury awarded the student $220,000 in this case.
2	The court found that school officials had acted unreasonably because it took them five weeks to address the harassment. The court also noted that school officials failed to take actions other than speaking to the harassers.
3	This scenario is not based on a real case, but the scenario is a common one. In this situation, it may be difficult to prove peer harassment under Title IX. Applying the *Davis* decision, school officials knew of the harassment but were not deliberately indifferent. It is important to note that even if school officials did not do all that they should have, they still may not be found to be deliberately indifferent if their response was not clearly unreasonable. The third prong of the *Davis* test will be the

Scenario	Outcome
	most difficult to demonstrate. To illustrate, it is not clear whether the harassment in this case was severe, pervasive, or objectively offensive. It is also unclear if the harassment denied Sally her education. Therefore, it does not appear that there has been a violation of Title IX in this scenario. Nevertheless, school officials should still pay attention and respond to such incidents of harassment.
4	Whether the court applied the *Davis* standard or asked if school officials acted in "bad faith" or "gross misjudgment," it seems that school officials did take steps to address the harassment. Although it is questionable as to whether enough was done to address the harassment, some courts have only required that school officials take some reasonable steps to remedy the situation. Likewise, it could be found that school officials did not act in bad faith or display gross misjudgment because they did take steps to address the harassment.

Assessment

5 Minutes

Provide each teacher with a 3 × 5 card to assess their understanding. The teachers should complete the following phrases on the back side of each card:

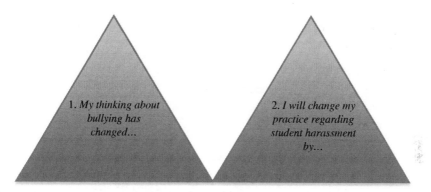

1. *My thinking about bullying has changed...*

2. *I will change my practice regarding student harassment by...*

Figure 5.1   **Harassment and Bullying Assessment**

FAQ

10 Minutes

As time permits, you may add some of these additional questions to the follow-up discussion.

1. The *Davis* case focused on Title IX. Isn't Title IX about gender equity?

Yes. Title IX prohibits sex discrimination at educational institutions that receive federal funds. The court has used Title IX in cases involving discrimination based on sex in both student-to-student sexual harassment cases and teacher-to-student sexual harassment cases. With teacher-to-student sexual harassment, plaintiffs do not need to prove the harassment was severe.

2. Is same-sex harassment actionable under Title IX?

Yes. The guidance from the Office for Civil Rights states that sexual harassment directed at gay and lesbian students is prohibited under Title IX. Specifically, Title IX prohibits harassment that is based on conduct of a sexual nature. Thus, it applies equally if someone is harassed by someone of the same sex or if the victim is gay or lesbian.

3. How do the courts define deliberate indifference and the other factors required to prove liability for peer harassment?

Prior to the *Davis* decision it was not clear whether school officials could be liable at all for peer sexual harassment. After the decision, there is much more guidance in this area. Although the *Davis* decision offers some guidance regarding the four factors discussed above, there has been some confusion in interpreting the precise meaning of the factors. For example, which school official needs to have "actual knowledge" of the harassment? Generally a school official, who has the authority to address the harassment, will suffice. Or what constitutes deliberate indifference? Some courts have found school officials to be deliberately indifferent when their response is "clearly unreasonable." What may be considered clearly unreasonable is not always clear, however. Finally, when is a harasser's behavior considered "severe, pervasive, and objectively offensive" enough to require action? When determining the severity, courts generally consider the totality of the circumstances.

4. Does Title IX apply in lawsuits where a teacher harasses a student?

Yes. In order for a school district to be liable for this type of harassment, the school officials must have known about the harassment and must have been deliberately indifferent in responding to the harassment. Even if the school is not liable, the teacher may be found criminally guilty for student harassment.

5. What is the legal standard when an administrator harasses a teacher?

Title VII of the Civil Rights Act of 1964 is the legal standard used in these types of cases. Title VII requires school officials to address the sexual harassment of employees. The sexual harassment against employees usually falls under quid pro quo harassment or a hostile work environment. Quid pro quo refers to giving something in order to receive something. For example, a teacher may be promised to be appointed department head in return for sexual favors. A hostile work environment refers to a severely hostile environment that interferes with a teacher's work performance. For example, when an administrator's sexual remarks are severe enough to negatively impact the working environment, the court would find a hostile work environment.

6. How can school officials avoid harassment in schools?

School districts should create clear sexual harassment policies that provide specific procedures. In addition to promptly dealing with claims of peer sexual harassment, school districts should implement preventive measures, and school administrators and their staff members should ensure that they know and follow those guidelines. To do so, school districts should clearly define peer sexual harassment in student handbooks and share the information with parents. These policies should be discussed to encourage students to report peer harassment immediately to the appropriate school official who is trained in the complaint procedure and has the authority to take corrective action.

In addition to handbooks, school districts should provide in-service sessions for faculty and staff members and hold assemblies for students to review complaint procedures. Within the training sessions, it is also important for faculty and students to learn what sexual harassment is, what it is not, what its effect is, and how to effectively respond to the harassment. Finally, lessons on sexual harassment could be incorporated into the curriculum. It is important not to overreact and to be conscious of the rights of the accused.

Supplementary Section

We anticipate that teachers may have several Title IX-related questions (e.g., athletics, single-sex classrooms) that were not covered in this lesson plan. Thus, we have included several examples of other frequently asked questions related to Title IX. Principals should use this supplementary section if time permits.

1. **Does Title IX encourage school districts to cut boys' teams?**
   No. Although some have argued that Title IX requires the elimination of male teams in order to achieve equity in athletics in school. Instead, facility limitations and budgetary concerns put heavy pressure on educational institutions to cut back their athletic programs, which in some cases results in the loss of male teams in order to move toward gender equity.

2. **May girls play on boys' teams or boys play on girls' teams?**
   Title IX allows separate teams for girls and boys but does not require it. Separate teams are often created due to differences in physical characteristics and sports preference. Under Title IX, school districts must offer equal athletic opportunities through separate or integrated teams. Although Title IX only allows girls to try out for noncontact boys' teams, states' Equal Rights Amendments usually allow girls to also try out for contact sports when there is no girls' team.

3. **What if the boys' baseball team gets new uniforms every year and plays its games on a nice field, but the girls' softball team only gets new uniforms every three years and plays its games on a run-down field?**
   This situation would arguably be a violation of Title IX. School officials would need to provide for greater gender equity between the two teams.

4. **Is instruction segregated by sex permissible?**
   Yes. The U.S. Department of Education adopted regulations that allow school districts to create single-sex classrooms and schools. In coeducational schools, both sexes must be offered equal educational opportunities and enrollment in a single-sex class should be completely voluntary. Single-sex schools are permitted, but a substantially equal single-sex or coeducational school for students of the other sex must be available.

5. **May school districts require pregnant students to attend another school?**
   No. The U.S. Department of Education has issued regulations under Title IX not allowing school districts to discriminate against pregnant students. Requiring pregnant students to attend a separate school would be seen as discriminatory.
6. **May gender be considered in hiring teachers?**
   Sometimes. Some gender-based discrimination is allowed under Title VII. However, there must be a legitimate reason for favoring one gender over another. For example, the school district may hire only a female teacher if the job requires supervising the girls' locker room.
7. **Who enforces that school districts comply with Title IX and how does enforcement work?**
   The Office for Civil Rights (OCR) in the Department of Education (DOE) is responsible for enforcing Title IX as it applies to schools receiving federal funds. The OCR has authority to develop policy on the regulations it enforces. Overall, the OCR has maintained a low profile in enforcing Title IX, which has led to girls and women seeking relief in the courts. Thus, in addition to the potential loss of federal funds via the OCR enforcement, schools that violate Title IX may be held liable for monetary damages.

   To ensure compliance with Title IX, three methods of initiating enforcement exist: (1) complaints, (2) compliance reviews, and (3) lawsuits. Under the first method, a person may file a complaint with the OCR alleging gender discrimination in violation of Title IX. The OCR then undertakes an investigation of the school. If the school is in violation and no settlement can be reached, the OCR audits the offending school's sports program and orders it to make any changes necessary to comply with Title IX.

   The second enforcement mechanism, compliance review, permits the DOE to perform periodic investigations of randomly selected public schools to verify compliance with Title IX. Although no complaint needs to be filed for the OCR to perform a compliance review, compliance reviews can occur after a complaint is filed.

   A final alternative enforcing Title IX compliance is to file a lawsuit against the offending school. Although lawsuits are costly and time-consuming, sometimes they are the most efficient way of bringing a school into compliance with Title IX for two main reasons. First, even after a complaint is filed, OCR is not required to implement a full investigation. In contrast, the filing of a lawsuit inevitably will result in an investigation by one or both of the parties. Second, the party who files a complaint with the OCR cannot receive monetary damages even if OCR determines that the school violated Title IX. Conversely, the plaintiff in a lawsuit can obtain monetary damages. Schools are more likely to comply with Title IX if noncompliance is punished with monetary damages.

Resources/Materials

Relevant Quotes

> Far from childish pranks, sexual harassment in the school setting consists of serious misconduct that can have a devastating effect on students at the receiving end.
>
> —Verna L. Williams (represented the petitioner in *Davis v. Monroe County Board of Education*, 1999)

Where the misconduct occurs during school hours and on school grounds, the misconduct is taking place "under" an "operation" of the federal education funding recipient. In these circumstances, the recipient retains substantial control over the context in which the harassment occurs. More importantly, however, in this setting the board of education exercises significant control over the harasser. The nature of the state's power over public schoolchildren is custodial and tutelary, permitting a degree of supervision and control that could not be exercised over free adults....

Whether gender-oriented conduct rises to the level of actionable "harassment" depends on a constellation of surrounding circumstances, expectations, and relationships, including, but not limited to, the ages of the harasser and the victim and the number of individuals involved. Courts, moreover, must bear in mind that schools are unlike the adult workplace and that children may regularly interact in a manner that would be unacceptable among adults....

Damages are not available for simple acts of teasing and name-calling among schoolchildren but rather for behavior "so severe, pervasive and objectively offensive that it denies its victims the equal access to education."

—*Davis v. Monroe* (1999)

While Justice Kennedy may have characterized this case as teaching "little Johnny a perverse lesson in Federalism," Justice O. Connor rejoined by saying that it "assures that little Mary may attend class."

—*New York Times* (Greenhouse, 1999)

The [*Davis*] standard has been set so high that it's a standard we can live with and in fact are living up to already.

—Julie Underwood, General Counsel, National School Boards Association

REFERENCES

American Association of University Women. (2001). *Hostile hallways: Bullying, teasing & sexual harassment in schools*. Washington, DC: Author.

Doe v. Board of Education of Prince George's County, 605 Fed. Appx 159 (4th Cir. 2015).

Davis v. Monroe County Board of Education, 526 U.S. 629 (1999).

Doe v. East Haven Board of Education, 430 F. Supp.2d 54 (2006).

Decker, J., Eckes, S., & Tanselle, L. (2015). Bullying, harassment of students with disabilities. *Principal Leadership*, 18–20.

Eckes, S. (2006). Peer sexual harassment and public schools. *Principal Leadership*, 6(5), 58–63.

Greenhouse, L. (1999, May 25). The supreme court: The overview; sex harassment in class is ruled schools' liability. *New York Times*. Retrieved from http://www.nytimes.com/1999/05/25/us/supreme-court-overview-sex-harassment-class-ruled-schools-liability.html

Long v. Murray Cnty. Sch. Dist., 2012 U.S. Dist. LEXIS 86155 (N.D. Ga. 2012).

Moore v. Chilton Cnty. Bd. of Educ., 1 F. Supp. 3d 1281 (M.D. Ala. 2014).

Vance v. Spencer County Public School District, 231 F.3d 253 (2000).

Title IX of the Education Amendments of 1972, 20 U.S.C. sec. 1681.

Title VII of the Civil Rights Act of 1964, 42 U.S.C. sec. 2000e.

ADDITIONAL RESOURCES

Alexander, K. & Alexander, M. D. (2011). *American public school law* (8th ed.). Belmont, CA: Wadsworth (See chapter 9).

Decker, J., Eckes, S., & Tanselle, L. (2015). Bullying, harassment of students with disabilities, *Principal Leadership*, 18-20.

Schimmel, D., Stellman, L., Conlon, C., & Fisher, L. (2014). *Teachers and the law* (9th ed.). Boston: Allyn and Bacon (See chapter 15).

Russo, C. (2009). *Reutter's the law of public education* (7th ed.). New York: Foundation Press (See chapter 13).

Chapter Six

Teacher Freedom of Expression

BACKGROUND

Although the U.S. Supreme Court has stated that neither students nor teachers shed their constitutional rights to freedom of expression at the schoolhouse door, school officials may discipline teachers for their expression under certain circumstances. The topic of teacher expression is important because teachers may not be aware that courts permit school districts to place limits on their speech—both in and out of school. For example, if a science teacher voices concern about the misuse of the school district's funds, the teacher's speech would most likely be protected since the teacher would be speaking as a citizen about a matter of public concern. However, when speaking about a private grievance, a teacher's expression will not be protected under the First Amendment. Also, this teacher's speech would not have been protected if she were found to be speaking pursuant to her official job duties.

Activator

Motivator

5 Minutes

The principal will distribute handout 6.1 to groups of teachers (six groups) who will discuss these scenarios. Teachers will return to these scenarios again after they have read more about the status of the law in this area.

Handout 6.1   Teacher Freedom of Expression Scenarios

1. A math teacher wrote a letter to a local newspaper, criticizing the school board's elimination of girls' softball. As a result of this criticism, the teacher was disciplined. *Did school officials violate this teacher's First Amendment rights?*
2. A special education teacher claimed that school officials retaliated against her after she filed a complaint with the state department of education. She noted that school administrators were not following special education law and failed to respond to her complaints about not receiving accurate lists of student caseloads. After she filed her complaint, school officials cancelled her extended contract. *Did school officials violate this teacher's First Amendment rights?*
3. A tenured elementary school teacher posted on social media that "after today, I am thinking the beach sounds like a wonderful idea for my 5th graders! I HATE THEIR GUTS! They are the devils [*sic*] spawn!" (A few weeks earlier a student from another district had drowned at the beach, and she was referring to this incident in her post.) None of her parents or students saw the Facebook post. The teacher was dismissed and claimed her First Amendment rights had been violated. *Did school officials violate her First Amendment rights?*
4. A nontenured teacher's contract was not renewed because she told her social studies class that she does not support the war in Iraq. The teacher claimed that her First Amendment rights were violated even though she had been told before to not give her opinion in class. *Does the teacher have a First Amendment right to tell her students that she opposes the Iraq War in class?*
5. After a nontenured biology teacher was advised not to discuss abortion, she was not reappointed after engaging the class in a discussion about the abortion of Down Syndrome fetuses. *Did the teacher have a First Amendment right to discuss this issue in the classroom?*
6. In California, a middle school dean posted obscene photos and comments on Craigslist. These postings were discovered by a parent in the district, who reported it to the administration. The teacher told the administration that he was seeking sexual relations with other adults and agreed to take the post down. *Did the teacher have a First Amendment right to post this information on Craigslist?*

As an alternative motivator, principals might choose to play the following YouTube clip: http://www.youtube.com/watch?v=l7ZHx2CzrR0

This news clip discusses teachers being disciplined for their controversial speech inside the classroom. The clip is nine minutes long, but principals only need to play the first few minutes. This short clip should be used to spark the teachers' interest about teacher speech. The clip could be followed up with a quick group discussion about the extent of teachers' First Amendment rights in public schools.

Rationale

3 Minutes

After a 2006 Supreme Court decision that found no First Amendment protections for public employees speaking pursuant to their job responsibilities, several court cases have addressed whether a teacher was speaking about an issue related to his or her job duties. In many of these decisions, courts did not decide in favor of the school employee because the employee was found to be speaking pursuant to an official job duty. Teachers need to understand the limits of the First Amendment in protecting and not protecting their rights to free expression inside and outside of the classroom.

Objectives

Post and/or state the following objectives for the lesson plan:

1. Teachers will be able to identify when their expression may be protected and limited under the First Amendment.
2. The teachers will be able to apply the First Amendment analysis to real-life scenarios involving teacher speech both inside and outside the classroom.
3. Teachers will gain new knowledge of likely consequences associated with unprotected speech.

The Law

15 Minutes

Teacher freedom of expression is a tricky subject. To develop content knowledge we advise that the principal ask the teachers to read the following information prior to the professional development session. Unlike other lessons in this book, more time will be allocated to the question and answer portion of the lesson. The principal should lead a discussion on what teachers were confused about in the reading, what they now know, and what they want to learn more about.

Handout 6.2   Teacher Freedom of Expression Reading

As a result of a 2006 U.S. Supreme Court decision, when teachers speak, pursuant to official job duties, their speech will not be protected under the First Amendment—even if they are speaking about a matter of public concern. Thus, a math teacher who complains to an administrator that the district places a disproportionately low number of minority students in gifted math classes might not be protected under the First Amendment (if the teacher is found to be speaking pursuant to his or her job responsibilities). If the teacher is not found to be speaking pursuant to job responsibilities, but rather is found to be speaking as a citizen about a matter of public concern, the speech may be protected. The U.S. Supreme Court ruled in *Pickering v. Board of Education* (1968) that teachers have a constitutionally protected right to speak about matters of public concern. Specifically, speech that is related to a matter of public concern is protected unless the speech is: (1) found to impair teaching effectiveness, (2) interferes with the relationship with superiors or coworkers, or (3) jeopardizes the operation of the school. In applying the *Pickering* balancing test, courts weigh the teacher's rights to freedom of expression against the school district's interest in maintaining an efficient school system. For example, in *Pickering*, when a teacher wrote a letter to the newspaper criticizing the way school district funds were used, the Court weighed the teacher's rights to free expression against the school district's interest in maintaining an efficient system. In making this determination, the content of the speaker's statement should be assessed to determine if the speech impaired one's teaching effectiveness or other factors. The Court did not find that Pickering's letter impaired his teaching effectiveness or other *Pickering* factors such as interfering with his relationship with superiors or coworkers, or jeopardizing the operation of the school. Sometimes it can be difficult to

(continued)

Handout 6.2   *(continued)*

determine whether the teacher is speaking as a private citizen or speaking pursuant to official job duties. For example, a tenured school psychologist's claim for First Amendment retaliation survived because he presented evidence demonstrating that he spoke out as a private citizen about a matter of public concern when he criticized curriculum changes for students receiving special education services (see *Koehn v. Tobias*, 2015). He had been discharged from his position shortly after making these complaints.

Teachers expressing themselves via social media have also been an issue in a few cases. A New Jersey appellate court upheld the dismissal of a teacher who posted on Facebook that "I'm not a teacher—I'm a warden for future criminals." The court noted that her speech was not related to a matter of public concern and was instead expressing dissatisfaction with her job. The court found that the teacher's speech did not deserve First Amendment protection (*In re Tenure Hearing of O'Brien*, 2013).

Whether on social media or not, speech that relates to a private grievance or has no social/political importance will not be afforded protection. For example, a high school teacher's recent statement that she wanted to bring a machine gun under a trench coat to school was not found to be protected speech. The teacher made this statement in the teacher's lounge after she had been reprimanded by her assistant principal for making inappropriate comments to a student (*Milo v. City of New York*, 2014).

Regarding expression that occurs inside the classroom, courts have generally upheld restrictions on teachers expressing their personal views. In so doing, courts have noted that teachers are hired to teach the curriculum. Thus, school boards may prescribe what will be taught and can restrict how it will be taught as long as the specifications are based on legitimate pedagogical reasons. In addition, school officials may restrict the use of certain teaching methods, if the teacher is given proper notice. Furthermore, teachers may not use their classrooms to promote their personal agendas. Thus, when dealing with controversial issues in the curriculum, teachers are expected to present both sides and encourage students to make up their own minds. Teachers have more freedom of expression outside of the classroom, but under certain circumstances, this speech may also be curtailed. For example, if a teacher voices her support for the legalization of marijuana on the local news, this teacher's speech could not be curtailed unless there was evidence that the speech impaired her teaching effectiveness, interfered with relationships of superiors or coworkers, or jeopardized the management of the school. Again, the content of the statements should be assessed in this situation. Although highly unlikely, it is possible in weighing these different interests that school officials might be able to curtail her speech if there was strong evidence that her speech jeopardized the management of the school.

It should also be noted that whether speaking inside or outside the classroom, nontenured teachers have fewer protections than tenured teachers. Specifically, tenured teachers are entitled to due process rights, making dismissal based on First Amendment concerns more difficult. Indeed, teachers should be knowledgeable about the legal parameters regarding speech both inside and outside the classroom and about the different consequences for tenured teachers compared to nontenured teachers.

Specific terms can be extracted from the reading and the Frayer Diagrams used in chapter 4 can be implemented.

Application/Content to Practice

20 Minutes

Ask the groups of teachers to revisit the real-world scenarios from the Activator/Motivator. Provide each group with the court ruling card that corresponds with the scenario they previously discussed. Give each group a few minutes to clarify their initial assumptions. Next, ask a representative from each group to read their scenario and the court ruling.

Handout 6.3   Teacher Freedom of Expression Scenario Ruling

Scenario	Court Ruling
1	The court found that the teacher was speaking as a citizen. The court also held that he was speaking about a matter of public concern and that his speech did not interfere with school operations. Thus, the teacher's speech was protected under the First Amendment (see *Pickering v. Board of Education*, 1968).
2	The court found that the special education teacher was not speaking pursuant to her official job duties and that she was speaking as a private citizen (see *Reinhardt v. Albuquerque Public School Board of Education*, 2010). The court noted that her job responsibilities did not relate to reporting any wrongdoing. The court also found that Section 504 of the Rehabilitation Act, which prohibits retaliation, protected the teacher in this instance.
3	It was determined that the teacher's posts were not protected by the First Amendment. With regard to her termination, the court found it to be too harsh of a punishment because she had an "unblemished" record with the district for fifteen years and was remorseful, and parents did not have access to the posts. She did receive a two-year unpaid suspension (*Rubino v. City of New York*, 2013).
4	The court decided that the teacher was hired to teach the curriculum and that she had no First Amendment rights to voice her personal opinions about the war in class (see *Mayer v. Monroe County Community School Corporation*, 2007). Of significance was that the teacher was told by school officials that she could teach arguments about Iraq from all perspectives, as long as "she kept her opinions to herself."
5	The court found that the teacher's speech could be regulated if the reason for regulation was related to a legitimate pedagogical concern. The court noted that this teacher had been provided with notice of what conduct was prohibited in the classroom (see *Ward v. Hickey*, 1993).
6	The case was not decided on First Amendment grounds, but the court found that this teacher could be dismissed because he was unfit to teach and because his conduct was immoral (see *San Diego Unified Sch. Dist. v. Comm'n on Prof'l Competence*, 2011).

Handout or present the following scenario and feedback sheet. Ask teachers to think about whether the teacher's First Amendment Rights were violated. After reading the scenario ask them to answer the set of questions provided.

Assessment

7 Minutes

The principal can lead a short discussion to ascertain the learning of the content. In so doing, the principal will stress that the French teacher's First Amendment rights were most likely not violated in the scenario below. Because it was a French teacher who complained about the cuts to the elementary foreign language program, she would most likely be perceived to speaking pursuant to her official job duties (instead of as a citizen). Therefore, the principal's decision to remove the French teacher from the department chair position and from the policy council would likely be upheld in court even though her comments were arguably related to a matter of public concern.

Handout 6.4   Teacher Freedom of Expression Assessment

A high school French teacher who was the chair of the foreign language department for her district wrote a letter to the editor of a local newspaper criticizing the district for cutting the elementary school foreign language programs. In her letter she noted that if the district had not been so irresponsible in the management of its funds, it would have been able to keep the elementary school foreign language program in place. In her role as chair, she met with the elementary foreign language teachers two times per year. After the letter was published, the principal of the high school assigned a new chair to the foreign language department and removed the French teacher from the school policy council committee. The teacher alleged that the principal violated her rights to free expression under the First Amendment when he retaliated against her for writing the newspaper article. Did the principal violate the teacher's First Amendment rights?

Question	Notes
1. Does this teacher have a valid First Amendment claim?	
2. Was this teacher speaking pursuant to her official job duties? If not, was the teacher speaking about a matter of public concern or about a private grievance?	
3. What if the teacher in this scenario had been a math teacher complaining about cuts to the elementary foreign language program?	

Had the teacher in the scenario taught math, courts would most likely not find the teacher to be speaking pursuant to his/her official job duties. Thus, a math teacher's comments would most likely be considered a matter of public concern and would be protected (unless the speech was found to impair teaching effectiveness, interfere with the relationship with superiors, or jeopardize the management of the school).

As time permits, you may add some of these additional questions to the follow-up discussion.

1. When are teachers' statements considered private grievances?

When teachers speak on matters of personal interest instead of a matter of public concern, their speech will not be considered protected. For example, one court found that it was a private grievance when a teacher complained about her over-crowded classrooms because she failed to link her argument to matters of public safety.

2. **When are teachers' statements considered matters of public concern?**

Speech will be considered a matter of public concern when it relates to political, social, or other community concerns.

3. **Do teachers have a First Amendment right to post material in their classrooms that expresses their personal viewpoints on controversial matters?**

Generally no. The courts have upheld the censorship of such materials because teachers are hired to speak for the school district, through the teaching of the district-approved curriculum, not to use their position as teacher to promote their personal views.

4. **Is it easier to dismiss a nontenured teacher for his or her classroom expression?**

Yes. In most states, nontenured teachers are not entitled to due process procedures unless they are dismissed during the calendar year. In most states, school officials may choose to not renew a nontenured teacher's contract without offering a reason. On the other hand, tenured teachers are entitled to due process rights, which could make dismissal much more difficult. It is important to note, however, that when school officials choose not to renew a nontenured teacher's contract, even though they often do not need to give a reason for the nonrenewal, school officials may not retaliate for a nontenured teacher's exercise of constitutionally protected speech.

5. **Can school districts offer additional protections to teachers to allow for greater freedom of expression in schools?**

Yes. School officials could craft district-wide policies that offer greater freedom of expression in schools. Also, some collective bargaining agreements may address this topic.

6. **Are there any state or federal laws that teachers could rely on for protections in these types of cases?**

Probably. Most states have adopted whistle-blower laws to protect public employees from retaliation when voicing concerns about illegal activity in the workplace. There are federal whistle-blower laws too. However, both state and federal whistle-blower laws are not as comprehensive as the First Amendment had been before the 2006 U.S. Supreme Court *Garcetti* decision. For example, Indiana's whistle-blower law states that "a public employer may not terminate an employee for reporting in writing a violation of law or misuse of public resources," but this law is limited to only appealing the disciplinary action. However, these laws vary by state.

In Wisconsin, for example, an employee "may not be retaliated against for disclosing information regarding a violation of any state or federal law, rule or regulation, mismanagement or abuse of authority in state or local government, substantial waste of public funds or a danger to public health or safety. An employee may disclose information to any other person. However, before disclosing information to anyone other than an attorney, collective bargaining representative or legislature, the employee must do one of the following [to] disclose the information in writing to the employee's supervisor, or disclose the information in writing to an appropriate governmental unit designated by the Equal Rights Division."

Regarding federal law, Congress has passed two federal laws protecting whistleblowers, but these laws would not apply to state employees. There are, however, other federal protections for claims of retaliation within certain contexts. To illustrate, under Title IX, school officials may not retaliate against teachers for complaints related to sex discrimination. Under the Americans with Disabilities Act and Section 504 of the Rehabilitation Act, school officials may not retaliate against teachers for complaints related to disability.

7. **How should teachers deal with the teaching of controversial material?**
Similar to the scenario discussed above, teachers should present both sides of the issue without inserting his or her personal viewpoints.

8. **Do teachers have complete academic freedom over their methods and materials?**
No, teachers do not have complete freedom. Courses in public schools are prescribed by the State Board of Education. Thus, teachers are not free to teach courses in a way that does not align with district requirements.

9. **May teachers wear political buttons in the classroom?**
Probably not. Although the U.S. Supreme Court has not addressed this issue, banning political buttons has been upheld by lower courts (see *Weingarten v. Board of Education*, 2010). Political issues and candidates can be discussed in a nonpartisan manner, but school districts can regulate teacher speech during school hours.

FAQ

10 Minutes

1. **May a teacher, as a parent, challenge the school district's curriculum?**
Yes. A teacher, acting as a citizen, may challenge school policies or curriculum and be protected by the First Amendment. This issue could get complicated, however, if the comment was related to the teacher's specific job duties.

2. **If a teacher voices her support for transgender rights on a radio show, may school officials discipline this teacher?**
No. This teacher would most likely be considered speaking as a citizen and about a matter of public concern. Thus, her expression would be protected unless the speech impaired her teaching effectiveness.

3. **What have the courts said about parental challenges to the curriculum?**
The courts have generally not allowed parental disapproval of instructional materials to dictate what is taught in the classroom. The school board maintains control over curricular material.

Resources/Materials

Relevant Quotes

Although the First Amendment's protection of government employees extends to private as well as public expression, striking the *Pickering* balance in each context may involve different considerations. When a teacher speaks publicly, it is generally the content of his statements that must be assessed to determine whether they in any way either impeded the teacher's proper performance of his daily duties in the classroom or … interfered with the regular operation of the schools generally.

—*Givhan v. W. Line Consolidated School District* (1979)

Our holding likewise is supported by the emphasis of our precedents on affording government employers sufficient discretion to manage their operations. Employers have heightened interests in controlling speech made by an employee in his or her professional capacity. Official communications have official consequences, creating a need for substantive consistency and clarity. Supervisors must ensure that their employees' official communications are accurate, demonstrate sound judgment, and promote the employer's mission.

—*Garcetti v. Ceballos* (2006)

The question of whether an employee speaks pursuant to his official duties is not always easy and *Garcetti* sets forth no dispositive test. Noting, however, that the test should be "a practical one," the U.S. Supreme Court states that formal job descriptions often bear little resemblance to the duties an employee actually is expected to perform.

—*Caruso v. Massapequa Union Free School District* (2007)

We specifically warned in our amicus brief in the *Garcetti* case that its implications were potentially far-reaching. The central flaw in *Garcetti* is the failure to recognize that often great public interest lies in giving government employees broad latitude to speak in the areas of their expertise. In a sense *Garcetti* got it backwards.

—Robert M. O'Neil, founder of the Thomas Jefferson Center for the Protection of Free Expression (Hudson, 2007)

REFERENCES

Caruso v. Massapequa Union Free School District, 478 F.Supp.2d 377 (E.D.N.Y. 2007).
Garcetti v. Ceballos, 547 U.S. 410 (2006).
Givhan v. W. Line Consolidated School District, 439 U.S. 410 (1979).
Hudson, D.L., Jr. (2007). *Garcetti's palpable effect on public employee speech*. First Amendment Center. Retrieved from http://www.firstamendmentcenter.org/analysis.aspx?id=18606
In re Tenure Hearing of O'Brien, 2013 N.J. Super. Unpub. LEXIS 28 (App.Div. Jan. 11, 2013).
Koehn v. Tobias, 605 Fed. Appx 547 (7th Cir. 2015).
Mayer v. Monroe County Community School Corporation, 474 F.3d 477 (2007).

Milo v. City of New York, 59 F.Supp.3d 513 (2014).

Pickering v. Board of Education, 391 U.S. 563 (1968).

Reinhardt v. Albuquerque Pub. Sch. Bd. of Educ., 595 F.3d 1126 (10th Cir. 2010).

Rubino v. City of New York, 106 A.D.3d 439 (N.Y. App. Div. 2013).

San Diego Unified Sch. Dist. v. Comm'n. on Prof'l Competence, 124 Cal. Rptr. 3d 320 (Cal. Ct. App. 2011).

Ward v. Hickey, 996 F.2d 448 (1993).

ADDITIONAL RESOURCES

Alexander, K. & Alexander, M. D. (2011). *American public school law* (8th ed.). Belmont, CA: Wadsworth (See chapter 15).

McCarthy, M., & Eckes, S. (2008). Silence in the hallways: The impact of Garcetti v. Ceballos on public school educators. *Boston University Public Interest Law Journal*, 17(2), 209–235.

McCarthy, M., Cambron-McCabe, N., & Eckes, S. (2014). *Public school law*. Boston, MA: Allyn and Bacon/Pearson (See chapter 9).

Russo, C. (2009). *Reutter's the law of public education* (7th ed.). New York: Foundation Press (See chapter 12).

Schimmel, D., Stellman, L., Conlon, C., & Fischer, L. (2014). *Teachers and the law* (9th ed.). Boston, MA: Allyn and Bacon (See chapter 9).

Chapter Seven

Teacher Out-of-School Conduct

BACKGROUND

The history of education in the United States is replete with examples of stringent ordinances and school-board regulations mandating a higher standard of conduct for teachers than for other community members. Such regulations were enacted because teachers are considered role models who hold a special position of trust and responsibility due to their relationship with the community's children. Even teacher's actions away from school are judged as if their conduct would set an example for how students should act.

In some cases, teachers have been dismissed from schools because of their out-of-school conduct. School boards often cite immoral behavior, unprofessional conduct, or unfitness to teach when teachers are dismissed for their out-of-school behavior during their private time. However, many teachers argue that their personal conduct outside of school is their own business. This lesson plan will address the circumstances in which school boards may dismiss teachers for their out-of-school conduct.

Activator

Motivator

7 Minutes

There are several different clips available on YouTube that discuss teacher out-of-school conduct. One very helpful clip can be found at http://www.youtube.com/watch?v=OECi-7JxCOc. If you are unable to access this clip, you can summarize the story.

VIDEO SUMMARY

In this clip, a biology teacher alleges that she was dismissed because of her part-time job. The teacher worked for a charter-boat company that took tourists out to catch fish. While on the boat, the teacher and the other female employees wore bikinis. School officials felt that this was inappropriate conduct for a teacher and decided not to renew her contract.

Principals will lead a discussion on the bikini YouTube clip based on the questions below (the questions still apply if teachers only heard the summary and did not watch the clip).

1. May school officials dismiss teachers for their out-of-school activities?
2. Was it appropriate for school officials to not renew this teacher's contract based on her personal behavior?
3. Are there certain types of out-of-school conduct that school officials should monitor more than others?
4. Are teachers role models for students? Do they teach by their behaviors in school and by their public actions outside of school?

Rationale

3 Minutes

School officials and teachers are often unsure about whether it is permissible to dismiss teachers because of their out-of-school conduct. This lesson plan will help clarify the law in this area.

Objectives

Post and/or state the following objectives for the lesson plan:

1. Teachers will be able to apply the legal standard to real-life situations that occur in U.S. public schools in examining discipline based on out-of-school conduct.
2. Teachers will be able to identify equal protection and privacy arguments in out-of-school conduct cases.
3. Teachers will be able to discuss trends in out-of-school conduct cases.

The Law

20 Minutes

Give the teachers about seven minutes to read the selection below. Then use the set of presentation slides to lead a discussion. See handout 7.2.

Handout 7.1   Teacher Lifestyle Choices Reading

Teacher Out-of-School Conduct

State statutes and/or collective bargaining agreements identify the reasons why teachers may be dismissed. Although the laws vary by state, state laws often include immorality, unfitness to teach, unprofessional conduct as well as incompetence and insubordination as reasons for dismissal. A school board must show cause in order to dismiss a teacher who has attained tenure. Specifically, in demonstrating cause, the school board must identify under what category of the state's teacher dismissal law a teacher is being dismissed (e.g., immoral conduct, unprofessional conduct and then provide evidence supporting the board's allegations).

Interestingly, there is no national standard about what constitutes immoral or unprofessional conduct. The interpretation of these concepts often varies according to state court rulings and community standards. Behavior that could cause substantial disruption in one community may cause little notice in another. In addition to state law variations, these concepts also vary over time. As the California Supreme Court observed: "Today's morals may be tomorrow's ancient and absurd customs" (*Morrison v. State Board of Education*, 1969, p. 226).

When employment decisions are based on a teacher's out-of-school conduct, the courts generally consider the notoriety of the conduct and the impact the conduct has on the individual's teaching abilities, when making a decision about the appropriateness of the action. Courts usually require evidence of a nexus (i.e., direct connection) between the teacher's conduct and impaired teaching effectiveness in order for the teacher's dismissal to be justifiable. For example, school officials might be able to discipline a teacher who is a stripper on the weekends if her stripping job became notorious in the community and had a negative impact on her teaching effectiveness. In dismissing this teacher, the school board would, of course, also need to identify a cause for dismissal (e.g., immorality or unprofessional conduct).

The Internet and social media has called attention to teacher's private lives outside of school as well. For example, in Georgia, a teacher was allegedly coerced into resigning after school officials learned about pictures on her Facebook page that showed her photographed with two glasses of beer while visiting the Guinness brewery while on summer vacation in Ireland. The teacher claimed that she had set her Facebook page to be private and that she did not "friend" students or parents. The teacher also noted that she was bullied into resigning and later filed a lawsuit against the district when it refused to reinstate her. A state court judge held that she was not entitled to relief (*Payne v. Barrow County School District*, 2009). Had this teacher not resigned, she would likely have had a successful lawsuit against the district because having a beer during summer vacation would not impair one's teaching effectiveness.

In the past, school districts tried to discharge teachers because of pregnancy or even divorce. Although a few school districts were successful in these types of cases, courts today do not support such dismissals based on their recognition that decisions pertaining to marriage and parenthood involve constitutionally protected privacy rights. Similarly, compelled leaves of absence for pregnant, unmarried employees also have been invalidated as violating constitutional privacy rights. For example, at least one court has held that offering a single teacher parental leave without a guarantee of her position at a nonprofit upon return violates the teacher's constitutional and statutory rights (see *Ponton v. Newport News School Board*, 1986). Likewise, a Florida court overturned a school board's termination of a teacher for lacking good moral character based on a personal romantic relationship (see *Sherburne v. School Board*, 1984). In this case, the school district questioned her choice as an unmarried woman to spend the night with an unmarried man.

It is also important to note that many teacher dismissal cases related to teacher out-of-school conduct never enter court. For example, a school district recently dismissed a teacher who had appeared in pornographic movies ten years before becoming a teacher, and the teacher did not challenge the school-board's reasoning that her prior conduct would have a negative impact on her classroom effectiveness.

School boards have an easier time dismissing teachers who have engaged in criminal conduct outside of the classroom (e.g., drug violations). In one case, a teacher was dismissed for possessing marijuana and for smoking it in his home. The school board relied on a North Carolina law that permits a tenured teacher to be dismissed for "nonmedical use of a controlled substance." The school board upheld his dismissal even though he was never criminally charged by the police (see *In re Freeman*, 1993). In another case, a teacher who brought a loaded shotgun and a loaded pistol to a local poolroom was dismissed for immorality (*Barringer v. Caldwell County Board of Education*, 1996). The court affirmed his dismissal because it found

Handout 7.1 *(continued)*

the teacher's conduct to be not only immoral but also highly dangerous. The court reasoned that the teacher's out-of-school conduct violated important principles that are required in the teaching profession. Similarly, an outstanding industrial arts teacher's dismissal was upheld after he was convicted of aggravated assault with a gun (*Skripchuk v. Austin*, 1977). And in Minnesota, a business teacher was dismissed for unprofessional conduct after being convicted for theft from a company he ran with two other teachers (*In re Shelton*, 1987).

In some cases, the State Board of Education may decide to suspend or revoke a teacher's license as a result of the criminal conduct. In a recent case, while her husband's ex-wife was in a car, the teacher used a hammer to break a car window and dent the doors. After a hearing, the state department of education decided to suspend her teaching license for over a year because the conduct was unbecoming of a teacher. An Ohio trial court reversed the decision to suspend her license because there was no nexus between her conduct and her performance as a teacher. The Ohio Appeals Court affirmed (*Wall v. State Board of Education*, 2015).

Most recently, lesbian, gay, bisexual, and transgender (LGBT) teachers have been under scrutiny in some school districts. In a California case, fellow teachers and administrators subjected an award-winning high school biology teacher to years of harassment and allegedly passed her over for promotion because of her sexual orientation. The California Court of Appeals found that a state labor law protected the teacher from harassment and discrimination based on her sexual orientation (see *Murray v. Oceanside Unified School District*, 2000).

Similarly, a federal court in Utah held that the removal of a teacher as the girls' volleyball coach was not justified by the community's negative reaction to her sexual orientation (see *Weaver v. Nebo School District*, 1998). The court noted that the community's negative response to her sexual orientation was not a job-related basis for her removal. Also, an Ohio federal court awarded a teacher reinstatement, back pay, and damages when it found that his contract was not renewed because of his sexual orientation and not because of his teaching deficiencies, as the school board asserted (see *Glover v. Williamsburg Local School District*, 1998). Some LGBT teachers who decide to marry and then face discrimination in schools might attempt to rely on the U.S. Supreme Court's recent decision on marriage equality. In this case, the Court ruled that the U.S. Constitution guarantees a right to same-sex marriage under both the Due Process and Equal Protection Clauses of the Fourteenth Amendment (*Obergefell v. Hodges*, 2015). However, this decision does not specifically protect teachers from sexual orientation discrimination in schools; only those teachers who live in the nineteen states with state laws would have such protections.

When school officials try to demonstrate a nexus between the teacher's sexual orientation and its impact on teaching in these cases, they will most likely be unsuccessful because of privacy issues and equal protection arguments. Specifically, discrimination against LGBT teachers has been challenged using the Fourteenth Amendment's Equal Protection Clause (U.S. Constitutional Amendment XIV, 1868) and some state statutes that grant specific protections to LGBT public employees. Under basic equal protection analysis, if a school district treats a gay teacher differently from a nongay teacher, it needs to demonstrate at least a rational reason for the different treatment.

In addition to the Equal Protection Clause, the Fourteenth Amendment's Due Process Clause may arguably provide protection for LGBT teachers. The Fourteenth Amendment requires that "no person be deprived of life, liberty or property without due process of law" (U.S. Const. Amend. XIV, 1868). As a result, certain types of governmental limits on individual conduct have been held to unreasonably interfere with important individual rights. This interference has amounted to an unreasonable denial of "liberty." Accordingly, there are certain protected zones of privacy (e.g., interracial marriage) where the government should not interfere.

Handout 7.2   Teacher Out of School Conduct Presentation Slides/Notes

Reasons for Dismissal

- Immorality
- Unfitness to teach
- Unprofessional conduct
- Incompetence
- Insubordination

A school board must show cause in order to dismiss a teacher who has attained tenure. To show cause means that school officials demonstrate a legitimate reason to dismiss a teacher. The legitimate reason will fall under one of the categories in the causes/reasons for dismissal list, which is established by the state.

When employment decisions are based on a teacher's out-of-school conduct, the courts generally consider

1. The notoriety of the conduct, and
2. The impact the conduct has on the individual's teaching abilities. Other factors courts might consider include the likelihood that the conduct will be repeated, the teacher's record, and any aggravating or extenuating circumstances.

Courts usually require evidence of a nexus between the teacher's conduct and impaired teaching effectiveness in order for the teacher's dismissal to be justifiable.

Protection for the Teacher

The privacy interests of the teacher must be balanced with the interests of the school board in all of the cases discussed above.
The Fourteenth Amendment's:

- Equal Protection Clause provides for the equal protection of laws.
- Due Process Clause requires that "no person be deprived of life, liberty or property without due process of law."

Application/Content to Practice

15 Minutes

The principal will split the teachers into groups of three to four. Each group will be given two or three of the six scenarios (the outcomes are to be folded over so the teachers do not see them; they are a resource for the principal during the Assessment portion). Within the discussion, the teachers should consider whether it would be permissible to discipline the teacher based on his or her out-of-school conduct. Also, teachers should consider whether there has been an equal protection or privacy violation.

Handout 7.3   Teacher Lifestyle Choice Scenarios

Scenario One:
An elementary school teacher was dismissed for immorality because he had a consensual sexual relationship with a seventeen-year-old high school student. He had taught this student when she was at the elementary school. The teacher argued that the student no longer attended the elementary school, that his conduct was not criminal, that the student went to school in another district, and that the relationship had not affected his professional duties. *Was the school board's action permissible?* consent law

school board

(continued)

Handout 7.3   (continued)

Outcome The State Supreme Court in Delaware ruled that the teacher was unfit to teach. The court found that the evidence demonstrated a "sufficient nexus between the undisputed sexual relationship and his fitness to teach." The court also found that the public disclosure of the relationship had a detrimental impact on the school.
Scenario Two: An art teacher painted different pictures using his buttocks. He posted a video of himself painting this way on YouTube. Although the teacher wore a disguise on the video, the school district still learned of this video and attempted to dismiss him. *Could school officials discipline this teacher?*
Outcome This teacher could be disciplined if his conduct became notorious in the community and had a negative impact on his teaching effectiveness. In this particular case, there was no impact on his teaching effectiveness and the school district ultimately settled the case for $65,000.
Scenario Three: An eighth-grade teacher from Oklahoma was planning to take his government class on a three-day field trip to Washington, DC. After a few of the parents learned that the teacher was gay, they demanded that the teacher not be permitted to chaperone the trip and that a straight teacher accompany the students. School officials removed the gay teacher as a chaperone, and he sued, claiming a violation of his rights to equal protection under the Fourteenth Amendment. *Does the teacher have a valid claim?*
Outcome Yes. School officials could be found to have violated the teacher's equal protection rights under the Fourteenth Amendment by treating him differently from other similarly situated teachers.
Scenario Four: A high school math teacher who also teaches the school district's driver's education course during the summer was arrested for driving under the influence (DUI). The math teacher was driving home from a school district holiday party. The school board would like to dismiss this teacher for unprofessional conduct. *May the school board do so?*
Outcome The school board would most likely be able to dismiss this teacher because his out-of-school conduct is related to criminal activity, and because he is the driver's education instructor. If he did not teach the driver's education course, it would probably be more difficult for school officials to dismiss him for his out-of-school conduct (even though it was criminal behavior) unless it was a felony. Teachers who are convicted of a felony may be fired without evidence that the serious crime impacts their classroom effectiveness.

Assessment

5 Minutes

Ask the groups of teachers to partner with another group that had a different set of scenario cards. Have the teachers trade the cards—keeping the outcome section folded over and out of sight. Ask individual teachers to pair up and have them report to one another what they think the outcome of the scenario is. Feedback about each scenario is provided by the outcome side of the card as well as the teacher partner who had previously discussed the scenario.

Scenario Five:

A teacher was terminated after photographs of her simulating fellatio with a male mannequin on a stage appeared on the Web. The pictures were taken by an acquaintance at a summer bachelor/bachelorette party and were posted without the teacher's permission. After some students learned about the photographs, they were removed from the Internet. The teacher was ultimately terminated because school officials believed the teacher had engaged in "lewd behavior," which undermined her authority and prevented her from being a proper role model to students. *Will this dismissal be upheld?*

Outcome

The Michigan Court of Appeals found in favor of the teacher, ruling that while the teacher's conduct might be considered "coarse," it was "not inappropriate for an adult venue." The court further reasoned that the teacher's actions did not otherwise "persistently and publicly violate important and universally shared community values" or demonstrate her unfitness to teach.

Scenario Six:

In Illinois a teacher was dismissed after being convicted of three misdemeanor counts of failure to file income taxes. This teacher made significant profits from commodities trading but did not file any income taxes. The teacher argued that this conduct was not related to his job at the school. *Will this dismissal be upheld?*

Outcome

Upholding the circuit court's decision, the state appellate court found that the conviction harmed the teacher's reputation and credibility as a teacher. The court reasoned that he could no longer function as a role model (*McCullough v. Illinois State Board of Education*, 1990).

FAQ

As time permits, you may add some of these additional questions to the follow-up discussion.

10 Minutes

1. **Can teachers be dismissed because of rumors of immoral conduct?**
   No. Teachers can only be dismissed based on factual evidence. At least one court has noted that disciplining a teacher based merely on allegations would create a dangerous precedent (see *Fisher v. Snyder*, 1973).
2. **Could a teacher be disciplined for encouraging a student to lie?**
   Yes. One court upheld the school's decision to discipline a teacher when he had a student lie about his weight at a wrestling tournament. Such conduct would probably be considered immoral.
3. **How do courts define immoral conduct?**
   Immorality or immoral conduct has been defined in several different ways. One court noted that "immorality is an imprecise word which means different things to different people. In essence, it connotes conduct not in conformity with accepted principles of right and wrong behavior. It is contrary to the moral code of the community; wicked; especially, not in conformity with the acceptable standards of proper sexual behavior" (*Harry v. Marion City Board of Education*, 1998).

4. **Could a teacher be dismissed for having a sexual relationship with a former student who has recently graduated?**
   Most likely. Some courts have permitted the dismissal of a teacher for such relationships. For example, in one case a high school teacher alleged that school officials violated her rights to privacy and intimate association when they denied her tenure after she engaged in an intimate relationship with a former female student. Affirming the federal district court opinion, the Sixth Circuit held that the school board acted reasonably (see *Flaskamp v. Dearborn Public Schools*, 2004). It would seem that the closer to graduation the relationship began, the more problems a teacher would have defending the relationship.

5. **Could a teacher be dismissed for having a nonsexual relationship with a student?**
   Possibly. Recently in Indiana a teacher lost her job because she forged too close a friendship with a middle school student. The student's mother complained that they commonly gossiped on the phone for hours about students' sexual lives and other inappropriate topics. This teacher had been warned by school officials about previous close relationships with students and ignored the warnings.

6. **May school officials punish a teacher for a posting a picture of herself smoking and drinking a beer on Facebook?**
   Maybe. Although the teacher may argue that what she does in her private life may not be regulated by school officials, the school officials might still be able to demonstrate that the picture has impaired her teaching effectiveness in the classroom.

7. **May school officials discipline a teacher for attending a rally to legalize marijuana?**
   No. Although teachers have the right to engage in political activities, school officials have substantial authority to place restrictions on teachers' political activities that occur inside the school. Activities that occur outside the school, such as the example mentioned above, would be much more difficult to control. Courts have found that teachers have the right of free association and cannot be disciplined for nondisruptive political activities.

Resources/Materials

Relevant Quotes

> A rational nexus exists between a teacher's off-duty conduct and his or [her] duties as a teacher in at least two circumstances: (1) if the conduct directly affects the performance of the occupational responsibilities of the teacher; or (2) if, without contribution on the part of the school officials, the conduct has become the subject of such notoriety as to significantly and reasonably impair the capability of the particular teacher to discharge the responsibilities of the teaching position.
>
> —*Powell v. Paine* (2007)

> Immorality as a ground for dismissal must "negatively affect the ability of the teacher to carry out his or her required responsibilities" and that the teacher must have "actual or constructive notice of the moral standard in question," which is

satisfied if the teacher should know that the conduct is "universally condemned" or "would cause a strong negative reaction against him in the community."

—*Ross v. Springfield School District No. 19* (1986)

In order to dismiss a school board employee for acts performed at a time and place separate from employment, the Board must demonstrate a "rational nexus" between the conduct performed outside of the job and the duties the employee is to perform.

—*Rogliano v. Fayette County Board of Education* (1986)

If the state may require parents to relinquish their children to the influence of public school teachers on a daily basis, then surely it is reasonable for parents to demand that public school teachers adhere to standards of conduct consonant with the moral standards of the community, especially when such conduct is required by law.

—*Rogliano v. Fayette County Board of Education* (1986) [Dissenting Opinion]

While the school board may legitimately inquire into the character and integrity of its teachers, in reviewing the character of a teacher, a nexus between the teacher's conduct and the workings of the educational system must be demonstrated.

—*Thompson v. Southwest School District* (1980)

REFERENCES

Barringer v. Caldwell County Board of Education, 473 S.E.2d 435 (1996).
Fisher v. Snyder, 476 F.2d 375, 377 (1973).
Flaskamp v. Dearborn Public Schools, 385 F.3d 935 (6th Cir. 2004).
Glover v. Williamsburg Local School District, 20 F. Supp.2d 1160 (1998).
Harry v. Marion City Board of Education, 506 S.E.2d 319 (1998).
In re Freeman, 426 S.E.2d 100 (1993).
In re Shelton, 408 N.W.2d 594 (Minn. Ct. App. 1987).
McCullough v. Illinois State Board of Education, 562 N.E.2d 1233 (Ill. App. 1990).
Morrison v. State Board of Education, 461 P.2d 375 (Cal. 1969).
Murray v. Oceanside Unified School District, 95 Cal. Rptr. 2d 28 (2000).
Obergefell v. Hodges, 135 S. Ct. 2584 (2015).
Payne v. Barrow County School District, Civ. No. 09CV-3083X (Super. Ct. Barrow Cnty. Ga. Oct. 15, 2009).
Ponton v. *Newport News School Board*, 632 F. Supp. 1056 (1986).
Powell v. Paine, 655 S.E.2d 204, 209 (W. Va. 2007).
Rogliano v. Fayette County Board of Education, 347 S.E.2d 220 (1986).
Ross v. Springfield School District No. 19, 716 P.2d 724 (1986).
Sherburne v. School Board, 455 So.2d 1057 (Fla. Dist. Ct. App. 1984).
Skripchuk v. Austin, 379 A.2d 1142 (Del. 1977).
Thompson v. Southwest School District, 483 F. Supp. 1170 (1980).
U.S. Constitutional Amendment XIV, 1868.
Wall v. State Board of Education, 29 N.E.3d 1024 (Ohio App. 2015).
Weaver v. Nebo School District, 29 F.Supp.2d 1279 (1998).

ADDITIONAL RESOURCES

Alexander, K., & Alexander, M. D. (2011). *American public school law* (8th ed.). Belmont, CA: Wadsworth (See chapter 15).

Eckes, S., & McCarthy, M. (2006). Teachers' privacy rights. *National Association of Secondary School Principals*, 6(3), 1–6.

Eckes, S. (2013, Sept.). Strippers, beer, and bachelorette parties: Regulating teachers' out-of-school conduct. *Principal Leadership*, 8–10.

McCarthy, M., Cambron-McCabe, N., & Eckes, S. (2014). *Public school law*. Boston, MA: Allyn and Bacon/Pearson (See chapter 9).

Russo, C. (2009). *Reutter's the law of public education* (7th ed.). New York: Foundation Press (See chapter 10).

Schimmel, D., & Stellman, L., Conlon, C., & Fischer, L. (2014). *Teachers and the law* (9th ed.). Boston, MA: Allyn and Bacon (See chapter 13).

Chapter Eight

Religion

BACKGROUND

There may be no constitutional issue in American life more controversial and divisive than the inclusion or prohibition of religion in the public schools. For decades the controversy has divided parents, teachers, school boards, and the justices of the U.S. Supreme Court. Should public schools begin their day with a prayer for all students or for those who want to pray? Can school districts require a moment of silence for prayer or meditation? Can principals invite clergy or students to give invocations at graduation ceremonies? Can students or teachers organize prayer or Bible study clubs? Can public schools celebrate Christmas? Can students distribute religious pamphlets? Can school districts teach and even require courses about religion? And can school districts teach creationism or intelligent design in science courses? These are some of the controversial issues that are being debated today and are likely to continue to be debated in the years to come.

What does the Constitution say about these questions? When most citizens think about religion and the Bill of Rights, two phrases come to mind: "Freedom of religion" and "separation of church and state." Although neither of these phrases is in the Constitution, they are a popular way of capturing two phrases that *are* in the First Amendment. The Establishment Clause ("Congress shall make no law respecting an establishment of religion") has been interpreted by Thomas Jefferson to require "a wall of separation between church and state."

The clause concerning "the free exercise" of religion has been interpreted to guarantee freedom of religion for all citizens. But since no provision of the Bill of Rights is absolute, the questions to be resolved by the courts are: Should Jefferson's metaphorical wall of separation continue to guide us today? And if so, how high should the wall be in the public schools? Second, how much freedom of religion must be protected or at least tolerated in public school? This lesson will indicate how the courts have ruled on these important questions and outline court opinions that can guide educators in responding to these sensitive issues.

Activator

Motivator

7 Minutes   Ask teachers individually to indicate their opinion about the following proposals or activities in Yourtown: Are they constitutional? Unconstitutional? You may choose to formally or informally tally the participants' responses.

Handout 8.1   Religion Hypothetical Cases

Hypothetical Cases	Constitutional?		
CASE #1: The principal of an elementary school invites student volunteers to lead the following nondenominational prayer at lunch time over the cafeteria PA system for students who wish to participate: "God is great, God is good, and we thank him for our food."	Yes	No	Don't Know
CASE #2: The school board proposes that every school in the district begin the school day with "one minute of silence for prayer or meditation."	Yes	No	Don't Know
CASE #3: The high school principal proposes that each year different community clergy give invocations at the high school graduation. He adds that no student will be required to participate.	Yes	No	Don't Know
CASE #4: A group of students petition the administration to recognize their prayer and bible study organization as an official school extracurricular club that will be eligible to publicize their meetings on school bulletin boards and daily announcements and to use school facilities for their activities.	Yes	No	Don't Know
CASE #5: The music teacher proposes a Christmas assembly at which the school choir would sing the traditional hymns of the holiday season such as "Silent Night" and "Joy to the World."	Yes	No	Don't Know
CASE #6: The school board issues a new policy that science teachers who teach about the theory of evolution must also teach students about the theory of creation science or intelligent design so that students can make up their own minds about these competing theories concerning human origins.	Yes	No	Don't Know
CASE #7: In order to teach an appreciation of different spiritual perspectives, the school board will require all high school students to complete a course in comparative religion (that will include readings from the Bible and the Koran) in order to graduate.	Yes	No	Don't Know
CASE #8: A group of fundamentalist Christian parents object to two required elementary school books: one is a popular novel that they believe promotes witchcraft; the second is a book that comments approvingly of gay marriage. Because the content of these books are in conflict with their basic religious values and beliefs, the parents make two proposals:	Yes	No	Don't Know

Hypothetical Cases	Constitutional?		
A. Both books should be eliminated from the curriculum because they are antireligious and/or promote the religion of secular humanism. B. If the books are not banned, the parents argue that compelling their children to read these books violates their free exercise of religion. Therefore, the students have a right to be excused from reading the books and be given alternative assignments.			
Case #9. On Valentine's Day, Sue Pious wrote on each Valentine, "Jesus loves you." Her third-grade teacher stopped Sue's distribution because she said that Sue shouldn't be promoting her religious beliefs in public schools.	Yes	No	Don't Know

As an additional or introductory motivator, principals might play the following YouTube clip: http://www.youtube.com/watch?v=nAJFpLn-zDs.

This clip discusses a Texas controversy about high school cheerleaders who want to include Bible quotes on run-through banners for their football team. The clip raises the question of whether the banners are school-sponsored or private student speech. The case is still being litigated, but the current resolution of this controversy is summarized in the Related Cases section below.

Rationale

6 Minutes

Teachers often wonder whether religion-related activities in class are legally permissible (e.g., singing holiday songs or student prayers). With an understanding of how the courts have interpreted the Free Exercise Clause and the Establishment Clause, teachers will be better equipped to know what is permissible under the law.

Objectives

Post and/or state the following objectives for the lesson plan.

1. Teachers will be able to identify how the courts have interpreted the Establishment Clause of the First Amendment in cases dealing with conflicts about religious issues in the public schools.
2. Teachers will be able to identify how courts have interpreted the Free Exercise Clause in school cases.
3. Teachers will understand the constitutional principles that emerge from court decisions concerning religion and education that provide guidelines for educators facing those issues in their schools.
4. Teachers will be able to explain the constitutional principles they support and better understand and respect the views about church/state issues with which they disagree.

The Law

15 Minutes

In this lesson, participants will investigate three elements of the law that directly relate to religion in schools: (1) the Establishment Clause, (2) the Free Exercise Clause, and (3) and the Equal Access Act. During this time, each teacher should individually make a KWL chart. The KWL chart asks participants to ask what they **K**now, what they **W**ant to know, and what was **L**earned. To begin, teachers will answer what they currently know and what they want to know (the first two parts of KWL chart). Next, each teacher should silently read the four-page "Religion and School Law" handout that is distributed. Finally, ask the teachers to complete the final portion of the chart. An example of the KWL chart is provided below.

Table 8.1

K	What do you **know**?	In other words, what did you already know about this topic before completing this reading.
W	What I **want** to know.	Before reading the four pages, list what you wanted to know about this topic.
L	What I **learned**.	After completing the four-page reading, list what you have learned.

After each teacher finishes the KWL chart, the principal will ask groups of teachers (three to six) to discuss the commonalities of their KWL charts. (*Note:* Principals should guide teachers to focus their time on K [what they know] and L [what they learned].) The principals should then have representatives from each group report out in order to determine the commonalities from the larger group.

Handout 8.2 Religion and School Law

> The First Amendment proclaims, "Congress shall make no law respecting an establishment of religion or prohibiting the free exercise thereof." But it is not obvious what these historic words mean. The answers can be found in the way the federal courts have interpreted the religion clauses over the years and applied them to disputes in the public schools.
>
>   In 1947 the U.S. Supreme Court for the first time determined the meaning of the Establishment Clause. In *Everson v. Board of Education of the Township of Ewing* (1947), all the justices agreed with Thomas Jefferson that "the clause against establishment of religion by law was intended to erect a 'wall of separation between church and state.'" Despite this unanimous interpretation, a majority of the justices did not believe that the wall of separation prohibited a school district from reimbursing parents for bus fare for transporting their children to religious as well as public schools.
>
>   Over the years, the unanimous support for a wall of separation among the justices began to erode. For example, in 1971 the High Court dropped the wall metaphor and established the following three-part Lemon test for determining whether a challenged government practice was constitutional: first, the activity must have a secular purpose; second, its primary effect must be one that neither advances nor inhibits religion; and finally, the activity must not foster an

excessive government entanglement with religion. In the *Lemon* case, the Court held that state salary supplements paid to teachers in religious schools violated the three-part test (*Lemon v. Kurtzman*, 1971).

In *Lynch v. Donnelly* (1984), Justice O'Connor developed the endorsement test that was a "refinement" of the test used in *Lemon*. This approach asked two questions: first, "whether government's purpose is to endorse religion" and, second, whether the policy "actually conveys a message of endorsement." In *Lynch*, Justice O'Connor explained that government endorsement of religion is invalid because it "sends a message to nonadherents that they are outsiders, not full members of the political community, and an accompanying message to adherents that they are insiders, favored members of the political community."

A year later the Court ruled on an Alabama statute that added the words "voluntary prayer" to a law that required schools to begin each day with a minute of silence. The expressed purpose of the law was "to return voluntary prayer to public schools." Therefore, the Court held that the statute clearly violated the secular purpose part of the *Lemon* test since its goal was "to convey a message of state approval of prayer" (*Wallace v. Jaffree*, 1985).

The following decade, the Court confronted the question of whether invocations and benedictions at public school graduations violated the Establishment Clause. In *Lee v. Weisman* (1992), a divided Court struck down the school-sponsored prayers and wrote, "If citizens are subjected to state-sponsored religious exercises, the State disavows its own duty to guard and respect" the diversity of religious belief. This is especially true in public schools where prayer exercises "carry a particular risk of indirect coercion." Similarly, in 2000, the Supreme Court ruled that it was unconstitutional for schools to authorize students to vote on whether invocations should be delivered before football games. In *Santa Fe Independent School District v. Doe* (2000), the Court explained that the Constitution does not prohibit an individual student from praying before, during or after school. However, the Establishment Clause *is* violated when a public school sponsors or endorses a religious practice, such as organizing an election to select a student to say a prayer at an athletic event. As the Supreme Court explained in an earlier case, the problem with such an endorsement is that "when the power, prestige, and financial support of government are placed behind a particular religious belief, the indirect coercive pressure upon religious minorities to conform to the prevailing officially approved religion is plain" (*Engel v. Vitale*, 1962).

In addition to prohibiting school-sponsored prayers, the courts also prohibit curricular proposals that promote religion. Thus the Supreme Court voided a law that required schools that teach evolution to also teach "creation science." The law violated the Establishment Clause because it advances a religious doctrine (based on the first chapter of the Bible) "by requiring either the banishment of the theory of evolution from public school classrooms or the presentation of a religious viewpoint that rejects evolution in its entirety" (*Edwards v. Aguillard*, 1987).

While the Establishment Clause prohibits public schools from encouraging religion, the Free Exercise Clause protects students in their personal religious expression. Thus individual students may say prayers in school and share their religious views with classmates as long as they do not cause disruption. Furthermore, the Free Exercise Clause and the Equal Access Act permit groups of students to organize religious groups in school. Congress passed the Equal Access Act to allow secondary students to form student-led, noncurricular clubs to meet during noninstructional time. The Act was upheld by the Supreme Court in the case of a Christian club that was denied the right to meet at a public school for Bible study and prayer. The school argued that recognizing a religious group would violate the Establishment Clause. But the Supreme Court disagreed and upheld the federal Equal Access Act that prohibited discrimination against voluntary student organizations based on their political or religious views. The Court noted that the proposed meetings were voluntary, student initiated, and not sponsored by parents, the school, or its staff. According to the Court, "If a state refused to let religious groups use facilities open to

(continued)

Handout 8.2 (*continued*)

> others, then it would demonstrate not neutrality but hostility toward religion." The Court further explained that "there is a crucial difference between government speech endorsing religion which the Establishment Clause forbids, and private speech endorsing religion which the Free Speech and Free Exercise Clauses protect. We think that secondary school students are mature enough and are likely to understand that a school does not endorse or support student speech that it merely permits" (*Board of Education of the Westside Community Schools v. Mergens*, 1990). Therefore, the Court ruled that the religious club should be allowed to meet.

Application/Content to Practice

In small groups, teachers will return to the nine hypothetical cases that were previously examined. The goal is to apply the principles and precedents of the Supreme Court's decisions to determine whether the activities proposed in the cases are constitutional and why. Each group will have one moderator, who will be given the table below to bring clarity to the discussion of each case. The principals should make enough copies of this handout to provide to every teacher at the conclusion of the activity.

20 Minutes

Handout 8.3   Religion Hypothetical Cases Answers for Moderator

Cases	Constitutional?	Why?
CASE #1	No	As the Supreme Court explained, it is unconstitutional for government officials to encourage or endorse a religious practice. Therefore, when a public school principal, who is a government official, invites students to say prayers, she is thereby encouraging religion and violating the Establishment Clause. However, as the Court also explained, students are free to say individual prayers at lunch or any other time before, during, or after school as long as they don't cause disruption.
CASE #2	Probably Yes	If the school board required "a minute of quiet for silent prayer," this policy would be unconstitutional since it would only encourage prayer, as the Supreme Court explained in *Wallace v. Jaffree*. But a majority of the justices have indicated that as long as the board does not state that its purpose is religious, and the only activity that is required is silence (for prayer *or* meditation), then students can use that minute of silence for any purpose they wish—whether religious, nonreligious, or even antireligious. Thus most moment of silence policies would be upheld if they have a secular purpose such as starting the school day with a time for silent reflection.
CASE #3	No	As the Court ruled in *Lee v. Weisman*, school-sponsored invocations or benedictions violate the Establishment Clause. The practice is equally unconstitutional if the principal asks a teacher, student, or parent to say the prayer, even if participation is voluntary. What makes this practice unconstitutional is that a public school principal, who is a government official, is promoting a religious practice. Instead, the government should be neutral concerning religion—neither endorsing nor inhibiting religion.

Cases	Constitutional?	Why?
CASE #4	Yes	Under the federal Equal Access Act, secondary schools that permit extracurricular clubs can't refuse to provide equal access to a group because of its religious or political speech. This would include the use of bulletin boards and other school facilities like any other extracurricular club. Discrimination against a student religious group would also be a violation of the Free Exercise Clause of the First Amendment.
CASE #5	Probably Not	How to handle Christmas in a public school can be a delicate matter. One approach is for schools to have "holiday," rather than Christmas, assemblies. But since Christmas is a national as well as a religious holiday, it is not unconstitutional to have a Christmas assembly where the school chorus sings the nonreligious songs of the season. The constitutional problem arises if the chorus only sings traditional Christmas hymns— which typically include explicit religious affirmations. In that case, there would probably be a violation of the Establishment Clause since such an assembly would appear to be an endorsement of religion. This does not mean that students can never sing or be taught about religious music. For example, such music can be taught objectively as part of a course on the history of Western music. But most judges probably would conclude that a program of religious hymns at a Christmas assembly just before Christmas would constitute an unconstitutional endorsement of religion. (However, the songs might be all right if they were part of a larger, objective curriculum about comparative religious celebrations.)
CASE #6	No	As the Supreme Court ruled in the *Edwards* case, such a policy would violate the Establishment Clause because it promotes a religious view, since it requires schools either to stop teaching evolution or to present a religious view that rejects evolution. Furthermore, creationism is based on the first book of the Bible and rejects scientific methods. Even though intelligent design is a more sophisticated theory than creationism, the proponents and goals of intelligent design are similar to those of creationism, and it has been rejected by a federal court for the same reasons (see *Kitzmiller v. Dover*, 2005).
CASE #7	Yes	The courts distinguish between courses and activities that *promote* religion, which is unconstitutional, and courses that teach *about* religion, which is permitted and can be required if it is taught objectively as part of the curriculum. Furthermore, reading and teaching about the Bible could be appropriate not just in a course on comparative religion but also in other courses such as literature, history, or music.

(continued)

Handout 8.3   *(continued)*

Cases	Constitutional?	Why?
CASE #8	A: No B: Probably Not	A. The parents have no constitutional right to require schools to ban books that are in conflict with their religious beliefs as long as schools have a legitimate educational goal in assigning the books. As one federal court explained, if schools were required to eliminate everything objectionable to every parent's religious views, this would "leave public education in shreds" (see *Grove.v. Mead Sch. Dist. No. 354*, 1985). B. In cases such as this, many schools choose to excuse students from classes such as sex education or reading assignments that are in conflict with their religious beliefs and, where feasible, provide alternative assignments. But most courts have not found "excusal" to be a parental right under the Free Exercise Clause since merely exposing students to controversial ideas does not interfere with the parents' freedom to educate their children in the religion of their choice.
CASE #9	No	Sue has a constitutional right to distribute her valentines with her personal message like any other student. The outcome would be entirely different if Sue's teacher distributed valentines to her pupils with the words "Jesus Loves You." This is because the teacher's valentines would constitute a government endorsement of religion that is prohibited by the Establishment Clauses. In contrast, Sue's individual religious views are protected by the Free Exercise and Free Speech Clauses of the First Amendment.

Assessment

5 Minutes

At the conclusion of the lesson, ask teachers to use the handout to individually record their responses on the two new cases below. Ask the teachers to discuss their responses with the person sitting next to them.

Handout 8.4   Religion Assessment

Case	Circle One	Decision and Reasoning
While Gail Good is saying her rosary prayers after lunch in the school cafeteria, her fifth-grade teacher quietly explains to Gail that she should say her prayers in church or at home but not in a public school.	~~Free Exercise~~ (circled) ~~or~~ Establishment Clause Principles	*she has the right to freely exercise during permition*
Sixth-grade teacher Sam Saint gives his students a flyer that announces a special Youth Prayer Service at a local church. He explains that all students are welcome but that they should get their parents' permission to come to the service.	Free Exercise or Establishment Clause Principles (circled)	*endorsing*

Answers:

1. The Free Exercise and Free Speech Clauses apply to Good's case. Based on these First Amendment provisions, Gail has the freedom and the right to say her individual prayers in school as long as she doesn't cause disruption.
2. The Establishment Clause applies to Mr. Saint. As a government official, Saint is prohibited from endorsing or encouraging religious activity in his role as a teacher. Since his distribution of the flyers announcing a prayer service is an encouragement of religion, it is a violation of the Establishment Clause—even if the parents give their children permission to attend.

Read each case and ask teachers to stand at a designated area of the room based on what they think about each case. For example, ask teachers that believe Gail (in the first case) can pray to stand in the back of the room. Have others stand at the front. Then ask volunteers to provide their rationale. Finally, use the answers provided to clarify any misconceptions. This can be repeated for the second case if time permits.

FAQ

As time permits, you may add some of these additional questions to the follow-up discussion.

7 Minutes

1. Must students salute the flag or recite the Pledge of Allegiance?
No. When children of Jehovah's Witnesses refused to salute the flag or say the Pledge for religious reasons, the Supreme Court ruled in their favor. If a majority of the voters want to require these patriotic exercises in schools, why should a small minority be free to ignore that requirement? In answer, the Court wrote:

The very purpose of a Bill of Rights was to withdraw certain subjects from the vicissitudes of political controversy, to place them beyond the reach of majorities and officials and to establish them as legal principles to be applied by the courts. One's right to life, liberty and property, to free speech, a free press, freedom of worship and assembly, and other fundamental rights may not be submitted to vote; they depend on the outcome of no elections. (*West Virginia v. Barnette*, 1943)

In subsequent cases, courts have ruled that any students can refuse to salute the flag and are not required to stand for the Pledge—even if they don't have any religious reason—as long as they are not disruptive.

2. Do the words "under God" in the Pledge violate the Establishment Clause?
The question has not been resolved by the Supreme Court. However, a federal appeals ruled that reciting the Pledge was constitutional. The court found that the Pledge was a patriotic, nonreligious exercise, and that the effect of the recitation was neither to advance nor to inhibit religion (*Newdow v. Rio Linda Union School District*, 2010).

3. **Can students receive religious instruction during school hours?**

   Yes. However, this "release time" instruction used by some communities must take place away from school and must not be taught by school staff nor paid for by the school.

4. **Can public school teachers do remedial work in religious schools?**

   Yes. In *Agostini v. Felton* (1997), the Supreme Court ruled that placing public school teachers in parochial schools to conduct remedial instruction does not necessarily result in "state sponsored indoctrination of religion or constitute a symbolic union between government and religion."

5. **Are there religious reasons to support church/state separation?**

   Yes. Since the plaintiffs in some prominent school prayer cases were atheists, there is a tendency to assume that those who support church/state separation are atheists, agnostics, or antireligious secular humanists. In fact, however, many religious people are "separationists." Historically, Roger Williams saw separation as a way to protect the churches against state control and "worldly corruption."

   Today, many believers fear that what government promotes and funds, government may control. As Justice Blackman noted in *Weisman*, "religion flourishes in greater purity, without than with the aid of government." Furthermore, religious sociologists have found that Americans are more religious than citizens of European countries where governments financially support churches and religious schools. Some conclude that the reason for greater popularity of religion in the United States is that since our churches can't depend on government support, they are more responsive, relevant, and creative than European religious institutions.

6. **Why are prayers permitted at presidential inaugurations but not in public schools?**

   While the Supreme Court sometimes seems inconsistent in its Establishment Clause decisions, the Court has always maintained a higher wall of separation in cases involving the public schools. This is because of the central and delicate role of public schools in educating our diverse student population, because students are compelled to attend, and because they are at a formative and impressionable age.

Related Cases

- In Bloomingdale High School, a student claimed that a 2 × 3 foot portrait of Jesus Christ, which had hung in the hallway for thirty years, violated the Establishment Clause. A federal appeals court agreed and ruled that the picture of Jesus in a public school clearly violated the *Lemon* test—its purpose and effect was religious and it involved an excessive government entanglement with religion (*Washegesic v. Bloomingdale High School*, 1994).

- In Texas, a high school cheerleading squad prepared run-through banners for the football team to charge through that featured quotes from the Bible. When the Freedom From Religion Foundation protested that the banners violated the Establishment Clause, school officials banned religiously themed banners. In response, parents went to court and argued that the ban violated the cheerleaders' freedom of religion and speech. As a result, the school board tried to resolve the case by adopting a new policy saying schools are not required to prohibit messages on the banners "solely because the source of such messages is religious." But the case is still in litigation (*Kountze Independent School District v. Matthews*, 2014).

- In a California case, a math teacher hung a series of large banners in his classroom with phrases such as "In GOD we trust" and "One nation under GOD" emphasizing America's religious heritage. When the teacher was ordered to remove the banners—because they promoted religion and were not relevant to math—he claimed the order violated his First Amendment rights. But the court wrote that the school did not violate his rights when it ordered him "not to use his public position as a pulpit from which to preach his own views of the role of God in our nation's history to the captive students in his mathematics classroom" (*Johnson v. Poway Unified School District*, 2011).

- In New Jersey, an elementary school student was prohibited from singing "Awesome God" in a voluntary, after-school talent show. School officials explained that because of its religious content and because it was "equivalent of a prayer," it violated the Establishment Clause. The parents argued that the school's censorship violated their daughter's First Amendment rights because the talent show was not school sponsored and because other students were allowed to sing and perform skits that reflected a wide variety of diverse views. A federal court agreed with the parents. The judge explained that by prohibiting the singing of "Awesome God," the school engaged in unconstitutional religious viewpoint discrimination (*O.T. v. Frenchtown Elementary School District Board of Education*, 2006).

Relevant Quotes

If there is any fixed star in our constitutional constellation, it is that no official, high or petty, can prescribe what shall be orthodox in politics, nationalism, religion, or other matter of opinion or force citizens to confess by word or act their faith therein. If there are any circumstances which permit an exception, they do not now occur to us.

—*West Virginia v. Barnette* (1943)

The First Amendment has erected a wall between church and state. That wall must be kept high and impregnable. We could not approve the slightest breach.

—*Everson v. Bd. of Ed. of the Township of Ewing* (1947)

The political interest in forestalling intolerance extends beyond intolerance among Christian sects—or even intolerance among religions—to encompass intolerance of the disbeliever and the uncertain.

—*Wallace v. Jaffree* (1985)

Families entrust public schools with the education of their children, but condition their trust on the understanding that the classroom will not purposely be used to advance religious views that may conflict with the private beliefs of the student and his or her family [because] students in such institutions are impressionable and their attendance is involuntary … Consequently, the Court has been required often to invalidate statutes which advance religion in public elementary and secondary schools.

—*Edwards v. Aguillard* (1987)

There are heightened concerns with protecting freedom of conscience from subtle coercive pressure in the elementary and secondary public schools. [What] to most believers may seem nothing more than a reasonable request that the nonbeliever respect their religious practices, in a school context may appear to the nonbeliever or dissenter to be an attempt to employ the machinery of the State to enforce a religious orthodoxy.

—*Lee v. Weisman* (1992)

The overwhelming evidence at trial established that ID (intelligent design) is a religious view, a mere re-labeling of creationism, and not a scientific theory … Encouraging the teaching of evolution as a theory rather than as a fact is one of the latest strategies to dilute evolution instruction employed by anti-evolutionists with religious motivations … ID fails to meet the essential ground rules that limit science to testable, natural explanations.

—*Kitzmiller v. Dover* (2005)

REFERENCES

Agostini v. Felton, 522 U.S. 803 (1997).
Banks v. Board of Public Instruction of Dade County, 314 F.Supp. 285 (1970).
Board of Education of the Westside Community Schools v. Mergens, 496 U.S. 226 (1990).
Edwards v. Aguillard, 482 U.S. 578 (1987).
Elk Grove Unified School District v. Newdow, 542 U.S. 961 (2004).
Engel v. Vitale, 370 U.S. 421 (1962).
Everson v. Board of Ed. of the Township of Ewing, 330 U.S. 1 (1947).
Grove v. Mead School District No. 534, 753 F.2d 1528 (1985).
Johnson v. Poway Unified School District, 658 F.3d 954 (2011).
Kitzmiller v. Dover, 400 F.Supp.2d 707 (2005).
Kountze Independent School District v. Matthews, 482 S.W.3d 120 (2014).
Lee v. Weisman, 505 U.S. 577 (1992).
Lemon v. Kurtzman, 403 U.S. 602 (1971).
O.T. v Frenchtown Elementary School District Board of Education, 465 F.Supp.2d 369 (2006).
Santa Fe Independent School District v. Doe, 530 U.S. 290 (2000).
Wallace v. Jaffree, 472 U.S. 38 (1985).
Washegesic v. Bloomingdale High School, 33 F.3d 679 (1994).
West Virginia v. Barnette, 319 U.S. 624 (1943).

ADDITIONAL RESOURCES

Alexander, K., & Alexander, M.D. (2011). *American public school law* (8th ed.). Belmont, CA: Wadsworth (See chapter 5).

McCarthy, M., Cambron-McCabe, N., & Eckes, S. (2014). *Public school law* (7th ed.). Boston, MA: Allyn and Bacon/Pearson (See chapter 2).

Russo, C. (2009). *Reutter's the law of public education* (8th ed.). New York: Foundation Press (See chapter 2).

Schimmel, D., Stellman, L., Conlon, C., & Fischer, L. (2015). *Teachers and the law* (9th ed.). Boston, MA: Allyn and Bacon (See chapter 11).

Chapter Nine

Student Records

The Family Educational Rights and Privacy Act

BACKGROUND

In 1974 Congress passed the Family Educational Rights and Privacy Act (also known as FERPA or the Buckley Amendment) to clarify who may and may not see student records. Congress passed the Act because of problems in the use of student records, especially the tendency of schools to provide outsiders with access to the records but to deny access to students and their parents.

The establishment of student records was originally a progressive development that enabled teachers, counselors, and administrators to have information about the "whole child," not just about grades and subjects studied. But the custom of allowing prospective employers, police, and other outsiders to see the records that were barred from parents led to abuses. For example, one mother was told she had no right to see records that resulted in her son being transferred to a class for the "mentally retarded." And a father who was told by teachers that his son needed psychological treatment had to get a court order to see all of his son's records. Furthermore, before FERPA was passed, most parents had little knowledge of what was in their children's records or how they were used, and the secrecy surrounding school records made it difficult for parents to assess their accuracy or to challenge erroneous information in the records.

Thus the goal of the FERPA was to correct these problems. However, some educators felt that the Act would cause more harm than good—that teachers wouldn't put anything critical in the records because they feared being sued for libel—and some administrators saw the Act as another unfunded mandate requiring unnecessary procedures and paperwork. In view of these concerns, this lesson clarifies what FERPA does and does not require and some of its consequences.

Activator

Motivator

5 Minutes

Ask teachers individually whether they think the following statements about FERPA (the Family Educational Rights and Privacy Act) are true/false or they don't know. The principal may want to formally or informally tally the totals for each case.

Handout 9.1   Student Records Hypothetical Cases

Hypothetical Cases	Was FERPA Violated?		
CASE #1: In order for teachers to have access to all of their students' records, FERPA requires that they must have permission from the principal (or his designee) or a parent/guardian of the student.	Yes	No	Don't Know
CASE #2: In order for a noncustodial parent to have access to their child's records, this person must have permission from the parent who has legal custody.	Yes	No	Don't Know
CASE #3: If parents believe that something in their child's records is false or misleading, the parents have the right to a hearing to present their evidence to challenge anything they believe is inaccurate.	Yes	No	Don't Know
CASE #4: Parents must be notified every year of their rights under FERPA.	Yes	No	Don't Know
CASE #5: A parent's consent is not required before schools share information from student records to protect the health or safety of the student or others.	Yes	No	Don't Know
CASE #6: Parents have the right to see teacher's personal notes about their children.	Yes	No	Don't Know
CASE #7: FERPA prohibits teachers from giving recommendations about their students to prospective employers over the phone without parental permission.	Yes	No	Don't Know
CASE #8: Teachers can be sued for defamation for critical comments they put in a student's records if the negative statements cause economic or emotional harm.	Yes	No	Don't Know
CASE #9: FERPA gives parents the right to file complaints with the U.S. Department of Education for failures to comply with the Act.	Yes	No	Don't Know

Rationale

3 Minutes

Issues of student privacy abound in the public school classroom. Teachers need a better understanding of how to confront these legal issues as they arise.

Objectives

Post and/or state the following objectives for the lesson plan:

1. Teachers will be able to discuss the main features of the Family Educational Rights and Privacy Act.
2. Teachers will be able to explain how the Act applies to teachers, students, and parents.

The Law

15 Minutes

FERPA has five important features. It is important for the principal to disseminate the information about these five features to teachers. Divide teachers into groups of four. Ask each group to read through all five features (provide groups with handout).

Handout 9.2   The Five Features of FERPA

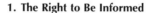

1. The Right to Be Informed

The Act requires school districts to inform parents of their rights under the Act each year. This includes the right to be informed about the kinds and locations of education records maintained by the school and the officials responsible for them. Usually, this information is included in a school's student handbook. FERPA also requires schools to effectively notify parents whose primary language is not English of their rights under the Act.

2. Protects Confidentiality

The Act protects the confidentiality of student records by preventing disclosure of personally identifiable information to outsiders without prior written consent of the parent. The consent must be signed and dated and include the specific records to be disclosed, the purpose and the individual or group to whom the disclosure may be made. Schools must keep a file of all requests for access including who made the request and why.

3. The Right of Access

The Act guarantees parents the right to inspect and review the educational records of their children. This includes the right to receive an explanation or interpretation of the records if requested. Schools must comply with a parent's request to inspect records "within a reasonable time, but in no case more than 45 days after the request" (*Code of Federal Regulations*, Title 34, Part 99 (2004)). Either parent (including a noncustodial parent) has the right to inspect their child's records unless prohibited by a legal document or court order.

Education records include any information maintained by a school (or a person acting for a school) that is directly related to a current student regardless of whether the record is in handwriting, print, tape, or computer file. The information may be in a teacher's or principal's desk as well as in an official file. However, FERPA does not give parents the right to see the personal notes of teachers, counselors, or administrators if these notes are used only as a "personal memory aid" and are not shared with any other individual except a substitute.

Exceptions: Consent Not Needed. There are several exceptions where student records can be shared without parental consent. For example, prior consent is not required when education records are shared with (1) teachers, other school staff, and administrators in the district who have "legitimate educational interests," (2) with officials of another school in which the student seeks to enroll (provided parents are notified), (3) with individuals for whom the information is

(continued)

Handout 9.2   *(continued)*

needed "to protect the health or safety of the student or other individuals," (4) pursuant to a court order, and (5) in connection with financial aid for which a student has applied (FERPA, 2000).

The Act requires each school district to adopt a policy specifying which school people have a legitimate educational interest in accessing student records. In addition, FERPA was amended in 1994 to explicitly allow schools to share information with teachers about disciplinary action taken against a student for conduct that posed a significant risk to any member of the school community.

If they wish, schools also have the option of sharing directory information from students' education records without a parent's consent. Directory information includes such facts as a student's name, address, email address, phone number, date and place of birth, dates of attendance, awards received, and photographs. Before releasing such information, a school should try to notify parents of what facts it considers directory information and their right to refuse to release the information. A school may release information about former students without trying to notify them.

4. The Right to Challenge

The Act establishes procedures through which parents can challenge a student record they believe is "inaccurate or misleading or violates the privacy or other rights of the student" (FERPA, 2000). In such a case, parents first should request that the school amend the record. If the school refuses, it must advise the parents of their right to a hearing where they must be given an opportunity to present their evidence and may be represented by counsel, at their own expense. The school must make its decision in writing based solely on the hearing and include the reasons and evidence to support its decision which is final. If the school decides the information is correct, it must inform parents of "the right to place in the education records of the student a statement ... setting forth any reasons for disagreeing with the decision" of the school (FERPA, 2000). The statement must be maintained by the school as part of the student's record. If the contested part of the record is disclosed to anyone, the parent's explanation must also be disclosed. This procedure includes the right to challenge an incorrectly recorded grade, but it does not give parents the right to contest whether the teacher should have given a higher grade.

5. The Right to File Complaints

The Act gives parents the right to file complaints with the U.S. Department of Education concerning failures to comply with the Act. The Family Policy Compliance Office of the Department has been established to "investigate, process, and review violations and complaints." After receiving a complaint, the Office notifies the school involved, and the school has an opportunity to respond. After its investigation, the Office sends its findings to the complainant and the school. If there has been a violation, the Office indicates the steps the school must take. If the school does not comply, a review board could terminate federal education funds.

Over the years, the Office has received thousands of complaints, and about 80% have been resolved informally. Furthermore, there have been over thousand formal investigations, but in no case has a review board terminated federal funds for noncompliance. Moreover, individuals cannot sue for violations; only the Department of Education has authority to compel compliance. In addition to enforcing FERPA, the Office staff will consult with teachers and administrators by letter or phone to answer questions concerning the Act and its application in specific school situations.

In addition to their rights under FERPA, special education students have additional rights concerning their records under IDEA (the Individuals with Disabilities Education Act). Because special education services often involve sensitive personal information, IDEA requires staff who use such information to receive training about confidentially requirements. Although FERPA allows schools to destroy student records at any time (except when there is a request to inspect them), IDEA requires schools to maintain IEPs (individual educational programs) and evaluations for at least three years to document compliance.

Application/Content to Practice

20 Minutes

Assign teachers into groups depending on the number of participants. The teachers will return to discuss the nine hypothetical cases that were previously considered. Each group could be provided three or all of the cases in table 9.1. Instruct the groups to come up with a decision and rationale based on the content they received in the previous portion of the lesson. After each group has an opportunity to discuss the cases, distribute the responses from table 9.2. Each group will have an opportunity to read the answers and perhaps modify their responses before discussing and clarifying any remaining questions in the large group.

Handout 9.3 FERPA Scenarios

True or False
1. **False.** FERPA does not require that teachers get permission from an administrator or parent before accessing their students' records. Instead, the Act requires each school district to adopt a policy indicating which school people have a "legitimate educational interest" in seeing student records. Teachers certainly have such an interest. If there are schools that don't include teachers among those having a legitimate educational interest in viewing the records of students they teach or advise, this is the fault of the school district, not the Act.
2. **False.** Custodial parents do not have authority to prohibit noncustodial parents from accessing their children's records. On the contrary, according to FERPA, noncustodial parents have the same right to access their children's records as custodial parents unless such access is prohibited by a legal document or court order. As one judge wrote, schools should make educational information "available to both parents of every child fortunate enough to have two parents interested in his welfare" (*Page v. Rotterdam-Mohonasen Central School*, 1981).
3. **True**. FERPA gives parents the right to a hearing to challenge any of their children's school records they believe are inaccurate or misleading. Even if the hearing officer concludes that the challenged records are not inaccurate or misleading, parents still have the right to place a statement as part of the disputed record about why they disagree with the hearing officer's decision.
4. **True**. FERPA requires that parents be notified each year about their rights under the Act, including their right to be informed about the kinds of student records kept by the school and how they can review those records.
5. **True**. A parent's consent is not required before the school can share information from student records with anyone if, in the judgment of school officials, the information is needed to protect the health or safety of the student or other individuals.
6. **False.** Parents do not have the right to see the personal notes of teachers, counselors, or administrators if these notes are only used as a personal memory aid and are not shared with anyone except a substitute teacher.
7. It **depends** on the facts of the case. FERPA only applies to student records. Therefore, if a teacher gives a recommendation (verbally or in writing) that is not based on information in the student's school records, FERPA does not require parental permission. But if the recommendation is based on the student's records, then prior parental permission is clearly required.

(continued)

Handout 9.3   *(continued)*

True or False
8. **False**, if the information is true. Truth is a defense to charges of defamation. Therefore, even in the unlikely event that critical or negative comments about a student's behavior in school caused emotional or economic harm, they would not be grounds for a defamation suit if true.
9. **True.** The U.S. Department of Education has established the Family Policy Compliance Office to answer questions about FERPA and to investigate complaints from parents (or teachers) about alleged failure to comply with the Act. Most complaints are about misunderstandings or misinterpretations of the Act and can be resolved informally. Where this is not possible and a school does not comply with the Act, the Office can order compliance.

Assessment

7 Minutes

For the ticket out the door in this lesson, ask teachers to list a few features of FERPA on a 3 × 5 card. On the way out of the meeting, the principal can trade cards; that is, teachers hand in their 3 × 5 card and teachers receive a card that summarized the five features.

Handout 9.4   FERPA Summary Cards

1. Inform. FERPA requires schools to inform parents of their rights under the Act each year.
2. Inspect. It gives parents the right to inspect and review the educational records of their children.
3. Challenge. It provides procedures that allow parents to challenge records they believe are incorrect or misleading.
4. Confidential. It prohibits disclosure of personally identifiable student records to outsiders without parental permission.
5. Complain. It gives parents the right to file complaints with the Department of Education if they believe that there have been failures to comply with the Act.

FAQ

10 Minutes

As time permits, you may add some of these additional questions to the follow-up discussion.

1. **What schools are required to comply with FERPA?**
   All public and private schools and educational agencies that receive federal education funds, either directly or indirectly.
2. **Who can assert their rights under the Act?**
   Only parents or guardians can assert their children's right of access and consent until they become 18 years old or begin attending a postsecondary school. After this, these rights can *only* be asserted by the student.

3. **Can students waive their right of access?**

   Yes. Individuals who apply to a postsecondary institution may waive their right to inspect letters of recommendation. Although institutions may not require such waivers, they may request them. These waivers must be signed by the individual student rather than their parents.

4. **Does FERPA apply to information about students that is not recorded?**

   No. Therefore, the Act does not prohibit teachers or administrators from disclosing information about students that is not recorded. However, sharing unrecorded *confidential* information with persons who have no need to know is usually unprofessional and unethical, might violate state privacy laws, and would be a valid reason for disciplinary action.

5. **Can parents sue schools for violating their FERPA rights?**

   No. FERPA does not give parents the right to sue schools for violating their rights. The Act is only enforceable by the Department of Education that can withhold federal funds from schools that have a policy or practice of releasing student records in violation of FERPA. However, some parents might still be able to sue schools where *state* laws prohibit disclosure of student records.

6. **Is a student's classwork or homework protected by FERPA?**

   It may not be. In a 2002 U.S. Supreme Court decision, Kristja Falvo objected to the practice of her children's teacher who had students exchange homework papers, grade them, and call out the scores which the teacher then entered in a grade book. Mrs. Falvo believed this violated FERPA. But the Supreme Court disagreed and ruled that the grade did not become an educational record until it was recorded in the teacher's grade book. According to the Court, if all classwork were considered an educational record protected by FERPA, this would impose a substantial burden on teachers and would make it more difficult for them to give students immediate feedback.

7. **What is included in a student's educational records?**

   According to FERPA, educational records contain information "directly related to a student and maintained by an educational institution." This is not limited to records concerning the student's academic program. Instead, courts have interpreted "educational records" broadly so that "parents and students will have access to *everything* in institutional records maintained for each student" (italics added) and used by the institution "in making decisions that affect the life of the student" (*Belanger v. Nashua*, 1994).

8. **Can teachers display student work without a parent's permission?**

   Yes, if it is not graded. Outstanding graded work can probably be displayed without permission under a school's Directory Information exception for student awards. However, if teachers want to display all graded student work, then permission should be obtained.

9. **If local police, who are investigating a crime, ask for information from a student's record, may schools share this information?**

   No, unless a parent has provided written consent or the police have a warrant to obtain that information.

10. If a high school student turns 18, do parents still have access to their child's records?

No. When students turn 18 or attend a postsecondary institution, the FERPA rights of access and consent will only be accorded to the student.

Resources/Materials

Relevant Quotes

> The plain meaning of the language in FERPA sets forth what educational agencies or institutions must do and not do in order to be eligible for federal funds. They must not have a policy which denies or prevents parents from having access to their children's educational records ... In addition, FERPA requires that the educational agencies or institutions establish appropriate procedures allowing parents access to the records upon request ... (FERPA) is intended to give (parents) the opportunity to challenge and to correct—or at least enter an explanatory statement—inaccurate, misleading, or inappropriate information about them which may be in their files and which may contribute, or have contributed to an important decision made about them by the institution.
>
> —*Belanger v. Nashua School District* (1994)

> While legal custody may be in one or both of the parents, the fact that it is placed in one does not necessarily terminate the role of the other as a psychological guardian ... [FERPA provides] that funds should not be available to educational agencies which deny to *parents* the right to inspect and review the educational records of their children. The regulations implementing the act allow inspection by either parent, without regard to custody, unless such access is barred by State law, court order or legally binding instrument ... Educators and school districts are charged with the duty to act in the best educational interests of the children committed to their care. Although it may cause some inconvenience, those interests dictate that educational information be made available to both parents of every school child fortunate enough to have two parents interested in his welfare.
>
> —*Page v. Rotterdam-Mohonasen Central School District* (1981)

> Under FERPA, schools and educational agencies receiving federal assistance must comply with certain conditions. One condition specified in the Act is that sensitive information about students may not be released without parental consent ... [The parents] construction of the term "educational records" to cover student homework or classroom work would impose substantial burdens on teachers across the country ... Even assuming a teacher's grade book is an educational record ... the grades on student papers would not be covered under FERPA at least until the teacher has collected them and recorded them in his or her grade book.
>
> —*Owasso Independent School District v. Falvo* (2002)

Excluded from FERPA's protections are records relating to an individual who is employed by an educational agency ... Although a [teacher's] file may contain "embarrassing or confidential information," the public interest in learning whether those who teach young children are qualified clearly outweighs her limited right to disclosure privacy.

—Klein Independent School District v. Mattox (1987)

The statute [FERPA] takes a carrot and stick approach: the carrot is federal funding; the stick is termination of such funding to any educational institution "which has a policy or practice of permitting the release of educational records (or personally identifiable information contained therein) of students without the written consent of their parents."

—Frazier v. Fairhaven School District (2002)

REFERENCES

Belanger v. Nashua School District, 856 F.Supp. 40 (1994).

Family Policy Compliance Office, U.S. Department of Education, 400 Maryland Avenue, S.W., Washington, DC, 20202, (202) 260-3887.

FERPA is found at Title 20, Section 1232g, *United States Code Annotated* (2000). Regulations for implementing the Act are in the *Code of Federal Regulations* Title 34, Part 99 (2004).

Frazier v. Fairhaven School District, 276 F.3d 52 (2002).

Klein Independent School District v. Mattox, 830 F.2d 576 (1987).

Owasso Independent School District v. Falvo, 534 U.S. 426 (2002).

Page v. Rotterdam-Mohonasen Central School District, 441 N.Y.S.2d 323 (1981).

ADDITIONAL RESOURCES

Alexander, K., & Alexander, M.D. (2011). *American public school law* (8th ed.). Belmont, CA: Wadsworth (See chapter 12).

McCarthy, M., Cambron-McCabe, N., & Eckes, S. (2014). *Public school law* (7th ed.). Boston, MA: Allyn and Bacon/Pearson (See chapter 5).

Russo, C. (2004). *Reutter's the law of public education* (7th ed.). New York: Foundation Press (See chapter 13).

Schimmel, D., Stellman, L., Conlon, C., & Fischer, L. (2015). *Teachers and the law* (9th ed.). Boston, MA: Allyn and Bacon/Pearson (See chapter 18).

Chapter Ten

Abuse and Neglect

BACKGROUND

Teachers will likely confront situations where they suspect that one of their students has been abused or neglected. In these situations, teachers are required to report their suspicions to the appropriate authority. In addition to their legal obligations, teachers are expected to react sensitively and appropriately when a student discloses abuse. Knowing the signs of abuse and neglect, understanding one's responsibilities, and learning appropriate ways of responding to children who disclose abuse are an important part of being a well-prepared teacher. This lesson plan will discuss teachers' legal obligations to report child abuse and neglect as well as how to detect and respond to abuse. In doing so, the lesson plan notes that different states have different standards of reporting.

Activator

Motivator

5 Minutes

In small groups, teachers will have five minutes to discuss the following scenario:

A student approaches you (a teacher) stating that her stepdad beat her with an extension cord because she would not get off her cell phone and refused to listen. The student is worried that if this gets reported, he will beat her again. Should the teacher report this suspected abuse and to whom? If not, why not?

The principal will guide the teachers to always error on the side of reporting. This case clearly needs to be reported. However, many cases of abuse and neglect are more problematic and nuanced. This will be a good lead into the rationale and objective for this lesson.

Rationale

3 Minutes

In 2013, approximately 679,000 children were victims of abuse and neglect. Sadly, the Children's Bureau found that 1,546 children died in 2014 because of injuries related to abuse and neglect (Children's Bureau, 2016). Teachers are in a position to help prevent abuse and neglect. In fact, teachers are considered mandatory reporters and must report suspected abuse and neglect.

Objectives

Post and/or state the following objectives for the lesson plan:

1. Teachers will be able to describe the reporting requirements for abuse or neglect cases.
2. Teachers will be able to recall the protections against defamation if no abuse is found.
3. Teachers will be better able to identify cases of abuse and neglect.

The Law

20 Minutes

The aim in this section is to help teachers understand how laws define abuse and neglect, how to identify cases of abuse and neglect, and when to report such cases. The principal should create two handouts or presentation slides to help teachers understand their role in defining and reporting neglect and abuse. The following handout table is provided for the identification of abuse and neglect.

Handout 10.1   Talking with Students about Abuse and Neglect

Take the child seriously, remain calm and reassuring, find a private place to talk, and position yourself at the child's eye level. Children who disclose abuse are likely to feel anxious and unsure of whether they will be believed. Giving the child a sense of comfort and control will facilitate disclosure.
Speak on the child's level, listen intently, use minimal prompts, and respond with the language that the child uses. Using general prompts, such as "Tell me what happened," allows the child to retain control of the situation and reveal only as much information as he or she feels comfortable sharing. In addition, responding using the child's chosen vocabulary helps to ensure that the child's credibility is not damaged; when children use language that does not sound like an ordinary part of their vocabulary, they are often disbelieved.
Obtain only the information necessary to make a report. It is likely that the child will need to repeat the same information to investigators and/or social service workers. Minimizing the extent to which a child must relive painful experiences is important.
Be responsive to the child's feelings while reassuring him or her that the abuse is not his fault, that you are willing to help, and that he or she is not alone.
Tell the truth. Let the child know about the process that you must follow, and do not make false promises. For example, tell the child if you will need to inform the proper authorities.
Thank the child for confiding in you. Let them know that confiding in you may have been difficult but that it was the right thing to do.

Talking with students about abuse or neglect from Association for Childhood International's Resource for Teachers (Austin, 2000).

Definitions of Abuse and Neglect

Federal law defines child abuse and neglect as "Any recent act or failure to act on the part of a parent or caretaker which results in death, serious physical or emotional harm, sexual abuse or exploitation; or an act or failure to act which presents an imminent risk of serious harm" (see the Federal Child Abuse Prevention and Treatment Act, 2003, n.p.). Although this federal law sets a minimum standard, each state then provides its own definitions of abuse and neglect and procedures for reporting. For example, Alaska's law defines abuse and neglect as "the physical injury or neglect, mental injury, sexual abuse, sexual exploitation, or maltreatment of a child under age 18 by a person under circumstances that indicate that the child's health or welfare is harmed or threatened" (Alaska Statutes, 2015).

State laws generally provide greater definition than the federal law, and they elaborate on the different forms of child abuse (e.g., sexual abuse, emotional abuse, abandonment). Unlike the federal law, which offers guidance, state laws are used to enforce child protection procedures. Due to the varying information within each state's law, teachers should consult the laws of their particular state.

In addition to state laws, individual school districts have also adopted policies focused on abuse and neglect. A typical school district policy from Lexington, Massachusetts, reads, "All LPS [Lexington Public Schools] employees who have reasonable cause or suspicion to believe that a child is suffering physical or emotional injury resulting from abuse or neglect shall report such a belief to the appropriate authority, according to the LPS *Child Abuse and Neglect Reporting Procedures*" (Lexington School Committee Policy, 2003). It is important to note that teachers only need reasonable cause, suspicion, or belief based on observations to report.

Reporting Abuse and Neglect

Most state laws outline the procedures for making a report of child abuse or neglect. A typical procedure would be for the superintendent and/or school board to establish reporting procedures in accordance with the law of the state. Whereas some school districts require the teacher to report the alleged abuse to a school counselor or school psychologist, other districts require teachers to report the abuse directly to the child protective services agency.

Also, in most states there are penalties when teachers fail to report abuse or neglect that they knew or should have known about. For example, in Ohio, a mandatory reporter who fails to report suspected child abuse can be found guilty of a misdemeanor of the fourth degree (Ohio Rev. Code, § 2151.99(C)(1), 2015). New Jersey's law is fairly typical in stating, "any person having reasonable cause to believe that a child has been subjected to child abuse or acts of child abuse shall report the same immediately" (New Jersey Statute Annotated 9:6-8.10, 2015).

Litigation has arisen when school officials fail to report child abuse in a timely manner. The Seventh Circuit Court of Appeals upheld a school district's decision to discipline a school psychologist who failed to report suspected child abuse in a timely manner (*Pesce v. J. Sterling Morton High School*, 1987). Likewise, in another case, a high school principal was convicted for violating the state's law of mandatory reporting suspected child abuse. Indiana law requires that abuse be "immediately" reported.

The court found that after the principal learned that a student was raped in the school, it took him over four hours to report it to the police or Child Protective Services (see *Smith v. State*, 2014). The Indiana Supreme Court affirmed his conviction of a Class B misdemeanor and his sentence of 120 days in jail.

There are also penalties for falsely reporting child abuse. However, if a report is made in good faith, the teacher will not be penalized even if an investigation determines that no abuse took place. Recently in Ohio, a parent alleged that a school official retaliated against him by filing a report with child protective services because the parent had advocated for his child with special needs. The court found that the parent had established a case of First Amendment retaliation and rejected qualified immunity for the administrator (*Wenk v. O'Reilly*, 2015). Specifically, there was some evidence that the administrator was motivated in part by the father's protected conduct of advocating for his daughter.

Identifying Abuse and Neglect

Whether a student directly discloses abuse or a teacher has reason to suspect that a child in her class is being neglected, teachers need to know what to look for and how to respond. The National Clearinghouse on Child Abuse and Neglect Information (NCCANI) has developed resources to assist reporters in identifying child abuse and neglect. Additionally, several scholars have written on the topic.

As noted by Saisan, Jaffe-Gill, and Segal (2008), physical abuse can manifest itself clearly in unexplained or patterned injuries, particularly those that seem age-inappropriate or have a pattern, as though made by a hand or belt. However, when there are no physical marks to indicate abuse—as in emotional or sexual abuse—behavioral signs or caregiver actions may help a teacher recognize an abusive situation. Behavioral signs can include fearfulness or shyness, inappropriate knowledge of or interest in sexual activity, destructive behavior, or extreme aggressiveness or passivity.

Of course, children could be exhibiting these types of behaviors for many other reasons; identifying abuse and neglect is indeed complex. Thus, when a child does not have physical marks but exhibits one or more of these behavioral signs, it would be prudent to discuss your observations with a specialist (e.g., the school psychologist). In addition to children exhibiting signs of abuse or neglect, the guardian or caregiver may show certain signs as well, including a lack of care for the child or a lack of interaction with the child, or they may seem particularly controlling or protective.

Disclosure of abuse can come in many forms. Children may confide in a teacher directly, disclose abuse to a friend, or reveal information through written or pictorial work. When this happens, teachers have an opportunity to provide comfort and support in addition to meeting their legal obligations. The above guidelines, adapted from the Association for Childhood International's resource for teachers (Austin, 2000), should assist teachers who need to respond to the disclosure of abuse and neglect. Above are suggestions for talking with students about abuse and neglect.

After an investigation, the appropriate agency might require several alternatives. For example, the family might receive services, there could be a court proceeding, or, in the worst cases, the child might be placed in foster care. Ultimately, there could be a termination of parental rights.

 Invite a local protective service worker or court official to discuss the identification of abuse and neglect and the procedures that are followed upon receiving a report. Provide the person with the lesson plan (especially objectives and readings) prior to the professional development session.

Application/Content to Practice

20 Minutes

In small groups, the teachers will discuss whether they should alert a school or childcare agency official about suspected child abuse. The principal will choose three to four of the following scenarios for the teachers to discuss.

Handout 10.2   Abuse and Neglect Scenarios

SCENARIO ONE
A student tells you (her teacher) that her volleyball coach has tried to kiss her on several different occasions after practice. You tell the principal what you learned, and she responds with "Oh, Emily … she loves to make up stories to get attention. Coach Pedo would never try to kiss her." You feel a bit uneasy about this conversation because you know the principal is very good friends with Coach Pedo. You have also heard other rumors around the school that Coach Pedo dated one of his volleyball players after she had graduated from high school.
QUESTION
Do you report this directly to a childcare agency official as possible abuse?
SCENARIO TWO
Larry is a first-grade student in your class. He was also in your class last year but was held back. Last winter, there were many days when it was below freezing that he came to school without a winter coat. Today, it was 10 degrees and Larry came to school without socks, in short sleeves, and his hair was still wet. You know his family has been facing hard times ever since his dad was laid off work. At the same time, you're worried that he is not being cared for properly. The other day, he mentioned that because he has to share a single bed with his two brothers, he usually ends up sleeping in the bathtub.
QUESTION
Do you report this to a school or childcare agency official as possible abuse or neglect?
SCENARIO THREE
You teach kindergarten. The children are given free time to play when they finish their morning work. During this time, Abby is playing with one of the dolls. When she thinks no one is looking, she moves toward a corner, puts the doll down her pants, and begins humping the doll. You have never seen this behavior before.
QUESTION
Do you report this to the school or childcare agency official as possible abuse or neglect?

(continued)

SCENARIO FOUR
Sixteen-year-old Heather has been a quiet student. One day her nose starts to bleed in class and some of the other students inexplicably laugh at this. When you approach her and start to write up a pass for her to go to the nurse's office, she tells you that her parents are Christian Scientists, and it is against the beliefs of her religion to seek medical help. The student further explains that she has not seen a doctor since she was born and that when she had a seizure last year, her parents simply prayed for her recovery.
QUESTION
Do you report this to the school or childcare agency official as possible abuse or neglect?
SCENARIO FIVE
One day, you accidentally brush against fourteen-year-old Shelly as you walk by her, and she jumps. You reach out to steady her by taking hold of her arm, and she flinches and looks nervous. After class, when the students are leaving, you casually apologize to Shelly for startling her. She waits until the classroom clears and then blurts out that she knows a girl who gets hit by her dad and that her friend's situation is making her jumpy. She then admits that her dad often hits her with his belt if she makes too much noise in the house. He tells her not to tell anyone.
QUESTION
Do you report this to the school or childcare agency official as possible abuse or neglect?

The principal can use the following table to lead discussions about each scenario. This can also make a good handout.

Handout 10.3   Case Scenario Guidance

Scenario	Principal Guidance
1 **Report**	You should report this to a childcare agency.
2 **Report**	It is always best to err on the side of caution, but in this situation it might be best to first discuss with the school social worker. Many school social workers have access to food, clothing and other resources to help families with financial needs. Alternatively, a teacher could report and allow officials from Child Protective Services to investigate. One of the outcomes may be additional resources for the family.
3 **Report**	Touching dolls sexually is one of the warning signs in identifying abuse and neglect. However, kindergarten students are also curious about bodies. In this case, it is more than touching, and it would be prudent to discuss with the school psychologist and perhaps to call Child Protective Services.
4 **Probably** **Not**	Probably not in the case of a nose bleed, but you should report in the case of a serious condition that might be life-threatening. Parents have a right to freely exercise their religion without government interference, but courts have permitted intervention when the parents' behavior puts the safety of the child at risk. In some cases, courts have found it unacceptable for parents to neglect a child because of religious beliefs and they have ordered medical treatment. These cases have come to be known as "religious-based medical neglect." Scenarios such as this one are difficult; however, it is always best to err on the side of caution and report.
5 **Report**	Although many parents engage in corporal punishment in home, it is still probably best to report this situation. Despite her request that you not tell anyone, you have a legal duty to report abuse.

Assessment

5 Minutes

Ask teachers individually to create a plan of action for how they will modify their interaction with students regarding suspected abuse of neglect. Specifically, ask teachers to write common scenarios of abuse and neglect they might encounter and what they will do about it. (*Note*: Do not allow teachers to discuss real cases in their classrooms so individual students discussed are not identified.)

Handout 10.4   Abuse and Neglect Plan of Action

FAQ

7 Minutes

As time permits, you may add some of these additional questions to the follow-up discussion.

1. **How can I find more information about my particular state's law regarding abuse and neglect?**
   The Child Welfare Information Gateway allows individuals to search each state's abuse and neglect laws. The list of state laws can be found at http://www.childwelfare.gov/systemwide/laws_policies/state/.

2. **If a child tells a school counselor about abuse in confidence, must the counselor disclose this information?**
   Yes. Teachers and counselors have a duty to report all suspected child abuse or neglect even if it was conveyed in confidence.

3. **Are teachers considered mandatory reporters?**
   Yes. All teachers are considered mandatory reporters because of their closeness with students. In addition to teachers, the following groups of people are usually considered mandatory reporters: doctors and health-care providers, social workers, childcare providers, and law enforcement. The Children's Bureau reported that in 2016 teachers reported more cases of abuse and neglect than any other group of professionals (Children's Bureau, 2016).

4. **Will a reporter's identity ever be disclosed?**

   Most likely not. All states require that abuse and neglect records be kept confidential. Currently thirty-nine states specifically prohibit the disclosure of the reporter to the alleged perpetrator. However, there are some circumstances where the reporter's name could be identified. For example, if a case proceeded to trial and witnesses needed to be identified.

5. **What should you do if your superior does not believe there is abuse or neglect and refuses to report it to the appropriate agency?**

   In this situation, a teacher must still report the suspicion to the local child protective service agency.

6. **Must you be convinced about the abuse before reporting?**

   No. Although the precise language varies among states, a teacher should report if she or he has a reasonable suspicion of child abuse. New Jersey's law is fairly typical in stating: "any person having reasonable cause to believe that a child has been subjected to child abuse or acts of child abuse shall report the same immediately" (New Jersey Statute Annotated 9:6–8.10).

7. **Can a teacher be penalized for reporting abuse that is not substantiated?**

   No. All states provide teachers with immunity if the report was made in good faith.

8. **Can a principal require you to contact the parents before reporting suspected child abuse?**

   No. If a teacher suspects child abuse, state laws require you to make a report. In one case, the principal was sued by the teachers' union when he wanted the teachers to first contact the parents. In the settlement, it was agreed that the teachers needed to report the suspected abuse to the appropriate agency (see Stoddard, 2015).

Resources/Materials

Relevant Quotes

> Schoolteachers, school officials, and school authorities have a special responsibility to protect those children committed to their care and control. School officials and school authorities, in particular, have special relationships with their teachers and direct control of the environment in which their teachers and students interact. When these persons are informed that one of their schoolchildren has been sexually abused by one of their teachers, they should readily appreciate that all of their schoolchildren are in danger. In no other context would we give even a second thought to the proposition that a school board has an obligation to deal with an instrumentality of harm to one of its students at school for the benefit of all of its students.
>
> —*Yates v. Mansfield Board of Education* (2004)

The purpose and intent of the statutory scheme is to encourage the prompt reporting of all suspected cases of child abuse. Blanketing mandated reporters with a presumption of good faith and imposing civil liability for a breach of the mandated duty to report further encourage the prompt reporting of suspected abuse. A determination that liability for a failure to report is dependent upon whether the charges are founded or whether the child abuse petition is ultimately sustained would contravene the statutory purpose of encouraging prompt reporting, and we decline to follow that approach. We conclude that a mandated reporter is obligated to report suspected cases of child sexual abuse based upon facts and circumstances within the knowledge of the reporter at the time the abuse is suspected and may be held liable for a breach of that duty even though it might ultimately be determined that the abuse was not committed or allowed to have been committed by a "person legally responsible" for the child.

—*Kimberly v. Bradford Central School* (1996)

REFERENCES

Alaska Statutes, 47.17.290 (2015).

Austin, J. S. (2000). *When a child discloses sexual abuse: Immediate and appropriate teacher responses*. Olney, MD: Association for Childhood Education International.

Children's Bureau. (2016). Child maltreatment 2014. Retrieved from http://www.acf.hhs.gov/programs/cb/resource/child-maltreatment-2014

Child Welfare Information Gateway. (n.d.). *Homepage*. Retrieved August 8, 2016, from http://www.childwelfare.gov/can/defining/federal.cfm

Federal Child Abuse Prevention and Treatment Act (CAPTA) (42 U.S.C.A. §5106g), as amended by the Keeping Children and Families Safe Act of 2003.

Kimberly v. Bradford Central School, 226 A.D.2d 85 (N.Y. App. Div. 1996).

Lexington School Policy Committee. (2003). Retrieved March 28, 2016, from http://lps.lexingtonma.org/cms/lib2/MA01001631/Centricity/Domain/201/LPS_SC_Policies/childabuse_rev.pdf

National Clearinghouse on Child Abuse and Neglect Information, at http://www.nsvrc.org/organizations/67

New Jersey Statute Annotated 9:6-8.10, 2015.

Ohio Rev. Code, § 2151.99(C)(1), 2015.

Pesce v. J. Sterling Morton High School, 830 F.2d 789 (7th Cir. 1987).

Saisan, J., Jaffe-Gill, E., & Segal, J. (2008). *Child abuse and neglect: Warning signs of abuse and how to report it*. Retrieved March 31, 2009, from http://www.helpguide.org/mental/child_abuse_physical_emotional_sexual_neglect.htm

Smith v. State, No. 18SOZ-1304-CR-297 (Ind. S. Ct. 2014).

Stoddard, M. (2015, June 22). Two educators who suspected child abuse say they were told to check with parents first. *Omaha.com*. Retrieved from http://www.omaha.com/news/crime/educators-who-suspected-child-abuse-say-they-were-told-to/article_acde0cce-d26b-5f00-a839-7a96bb271eb2.html

Wenk v. O'Reilly, 783 F.3d 585 (6th Cir. 2015).

Yates v. Mansfield Board of Education, 808 N.E.2d 861 (Ohio 2004).

ADDITIONAL RESOURCES

Alexander, K., & Alexander, M. D. (2011). *American public school law* (8th ed.). Belmont, CA: Wadsworth (See chapter 9).

McCarthy, M., Cambron-McCabe, N., & Eckes, S. (2014). *Public school law*. Boston, MA: Allyn and Bacon/Pearson (See chapter 9).

Russo, C. (2009). *Reutter's the law of public education* (7th ed.). New York: Foundation Press (See chapter 13).

Schimmel, D., Stellman, L., Conlon, C., & Fisher, L. (2014). *Teachers and the law* (9th ed.). Boston, MA: Allyn and Bacon (See chapter 7).

Conclusion

Teaching and Practicing Preventative Law

We believe this book will give principals the tools they need to avoid lawsuits by teaching their staff the information they need to practice preventive law.

This belief is based on two convictions: first, the principal is uniquely positioned and highly capable of being the school's chief instructor of preventive law. Second, school staff can be armed with the legal knowledge and skills that would enable them to avoid legal mistakes. As a result of these beliefs, we have created this set of legal lesson plans that principals can use to be conscious, informed and effective law teachers in their schools.

Continuing to neglect the issue of legal illiteracy can result in high costs—in terms of time and emotion as well as money. Principals have the authority and opportunity to design and implement in-service professional development programs in this critical area, which has been largely neglected in teacher preparation programs. Because of this neglect, most teachers gain their legal information from colleagues who are similarly uninformed and misinformed. That is why it is so important for principals to correct this misinformation and provide their teachers with the basic knowledge they need to be legally literate. Armed with this knowledge, teachers are unlikely to make the common mistakes described in these lessons, such as unintentionally violating students' constitutional rights or hesitating to discipline students because of unfounded fear of liability. Thus, as a result of these lessons, principals and teachers will avoid lawsuits by being partners in the practice of preventive law.

Appendix A

Finding the Law

The purpose of this appendix is to assist principals and teachers with finding free legal resources (e.g., case law, statutory law) on the Web. The following websites are easy to use and a great resource for school-law information.

FINDLAW

FindLaw is a free site that contains U.S. Supreme Court decisions, federal laws, federal decisions, and other state resources. The site also has a specific link to other school-law topics.

- To find the Education Law Section, go to www.findlaw.com.
- Click on View More underneath the Individual Issues link on the right-hand side. Click on Education Law under the Other Topics link.

This area has a frequently-asked-questions area, specifically related to school legal issues, an overview of special education law, and forms. You may also ask legal questions via e-mail.

- To find the Cases and Laws Section, go to www.findlaw.com/casecode.

In this section, you may search by case name, topic, federal laws, federal decisions, and you can find various state resources.

CORNELL UNIVERSITY LAW SCHOOL LEGAL INFORMATION INSTITUTE (LII)

LII is a free legal database that has U.S. Supreme Court decisions, federal laws, federal decisions, and other state resources.

- To find this site, go to www.law.cornell.edu.

In this website, principals and teachers can use various search terms to find federal laws, U.S. Supreme Court opinions, and some federal and state court opinions.

NATIONAL SCHOOL BOARDS ASSOCIATION (NSBA)

NSBA is a not-for-profit organization comprising state associations of school boards. The organization represents the interests of school boards in school legal matters. Also, NSBA distributes a weekly e-mail, which highlights the most recent lawsuits filed. Students, as well as principals and teachers, are encouraged to subscribe to the NSBA's Legal Clips via e-mail at http://www.nsba.org/legalclips.

- The organization's website address is www.nsba.org/site/index.asp.

EDUCATION WEEK'S SCHOOL-LAW BLOG

Education Week has an excellent school-law blog containing postings about cases, current events, and other items of interest.

- This particular blog can be found at http://blogs.edweek.org/edweek/school_law/.

This blog also links to other good school-law blogs, including *At the School House Gate*, *Principal's Policy Blog* (NASSP), the *EdJurist Accord*, and the *Special Education Law Blog*.

OYEZ

At this site, you may listen to actual U.S. Supreme Court arguments. Also available at this site is interesting information about U.S. Supreme Court justices, including a virtual tour of Justice Kennedy's chambers.

- The address for this site is http://www.oyez.org/.

GOOGLE

Searching on Google will also locate a variety of information; however, be careful that the information is not dated (and, therefore, no longer good law) or inaccurate. Google may be used to find state statutes. For example, by typing the "state name" and "code," most state statutes can be found.

Appendix B

Constitutional and Judicial Sources of Education Law

The three most applicable amendments to school-law cases include the following:

First Amendment (Religion, Speech, Press, Assembly, Petition)

- Congress shall make no law respecting an establishment of religion, or prohibiting the free exercise thereof; or abridging the freedom of speech, or of the press; or the right of the people peaceably to assemble, and to petition the government for a redress of grievances.

Fourth Amendment (Search and Seizure)

- The right of the people to be secure in their persons, houses, papers, and effects, against unreasonable searches and seizures, shall not be violated, and no warrants shall issue, but upon probable cause, supported by oath or affirmation, and particularly describing the place to be searched, and the persons or things to be seized.

Fourteenth Amendment (Due Process, Equal Protection)

- Section 1. All persons born or naturalized in the United States, and subject to the jurisdiction thereof, are citizens of the United States and of the state wherein they reside. No state shall make or enforce any law which shall abridge the privileges or immunities of citizens of the United States; nor shall any state deprive any person of life, liberty, or property, without due process of law; nor deny to any person within its jurisdiction the equal protection of the laws.

Appendix C

The Court System

STATE COURTS

The state court system has three levels: trial courts (usually called circuit, superior, or district courts), appeals courts, and a state supreme court. States use different terminology to describe the three levels. Plaintiffs may file their lawsuits in state court or in federal court (if there is a federal issue involved).

FEDERAL COURTS

The federal court system also has three levels: district court, circuit court of appeals, and U.S. Supreme Court.

DISTRICT COURTS

There are ninety-four district courts in the United States. Decisions from a district court can be reviewed in the court of appeals for the circuit in which the district is included. For example, if a federal district court case from Indiana is appealed, the case would be heard in the Seventh Circuit Court of Appeals. All federal judges have lifetime appointments.

COURTS OF APPEALS

There are thirteen courts of appeals. The courts of appeals usually hear and decide cases in three-judge panels. The courts of appeals are listed below.

- *First Circuit:* Maine, Massachusetts, New Hampshire, Puerto Rico, Rhode Island
- *Second Circuit:* Connecticut, New York, Vermont

- *Third Circuit:* Delaware, New Jersey, Pennsylvania, Virgin Islands
- *Fourth Circuit:* Maryland, North Carolina, South Carolina, Virginia, West Virginia
- *Fifth Circuit:* District of Canal Zone, Louisiana, Mississippi, Texas
- *Sixth Circuit:* Kentucky, Michigan, Ohio, Tennessee
- *Seventh Circuit:* Illinois, Indiana, Wisconsin
- *Eighth Circuit:* Arkansas, Iowa, Minnesota, Missouri, Nebraska, North Dakota, South Dakota
- *Ninth Circuit:* Alaska, Arizona, California, Guam, Hawaii, Idaho, Montana, Nevada, Oregon, Washington
- *Tenth Circuit:* Colorado, Kansas, New Mexico, Oklahoma, Utah, Wyoming
- *Eleventh Circuit:* Alabama, Florida, Georgia
- *Federal Circuit:* All federal judicial decisions that relate to a specialized area
- *District of Columbia:* District of Columbia

SUPREME COURT

This court has nine justices, one of whom is the Chief Justice. The Supreme Court sits in Washington, D.C. The Supreme Court hears less than 5 percent of the cases it is asked to hear each year. The current members of the Court are John Roberts (Chief Justice), John Paul Stevens, Samuel Alito, Ruth Bader Ginsburg, Clarence Thomas, Stephen Breyer, Sonia Sotomayor, and Anthony Kennedy. The Supreme Court justices have lifetime appointments. As of this publication date, no one has been appointed and confirmed by the Senate to replace Justice Antonin Scalia, who died in 2016.

Index

About the Authors

David Schimmel, J.D., is professor emeritus at the University of Massachusetts, Amherst, and from 1999 to 2010 was visiting professor at Harvard University's Graduate School of Education. He is author of over seventy articles and coauthor of eight books about law and education, including *Teachers and the Law*, 9th edition (2015). Professor Schimmel is a recipient of the Education Press Association of America's Distinguished Achievement Award for Excellence in Educational Journalism and the Education Law Association's McGhehey (lifetime achievement) Award. After graduating from Yale Law School, he briefly practiced law, was an Army Infantry Officer, and served on the Peace Corps staff for six years before starting his teaching career at UMass. His current teaching, research and writing focus is on promoting legal literacy for teachers.

Suzanne Eckes, J.D., Ph.D., is a professor in the Educational Leadership and Policy Studies Department at Indiana University. Dr. Eckes has published over one hundred school-law articles and book chapters, is a coeditor of the *Principal's Legal Handbook*, *Contemporary Legal Issues in Higher Education*, and *School Discipline and Safety*, and is a coauthor of the school law books *Legal Rights of Teachers and Students* and *Public School Law*. She is the president-elect of the Education Law Association and a legal contributor to the National Association of Secondary School Principals' monthly magazine. Prior to joining the faculty at Indiana University, Professor Eckes was a high school French teacher in the Mississippi Delta region and an attorney at a Chicago law firm. She continues to work as an expert witness in education-related litigation. She earned her master's in Education from Harvard University and both her law degree and Ph.D. from the University of Wisconsin–Madison.

Matthew Militello, Ph.D., is the Wells Fargo Distinguished Professor in Educational Leadership at East Carolina University. He has held faculty positions at North Carolina State University (2008–2014) and the University of Massachusetts at Amherst (2005–2008). Prior to his academic career, Militello was a middle and high public school teacher, assistant principal, and principal in Michigan (1992–2003).

Professor Militello has more than sixty publications including coauthoring five books: *Reframing Community Partnerships in Education: Uniting the Power of Place and Wisdom of People* (2016); *How to Prevent Special Education Litigation: Eight Legal Lesson Plans* (2015); *Principal 2.0: Technology and Educational Leadership* (2013); *Principals Teaching the Law: 10 Legal Lessons Your Teachers Must Know* (2010); and *Leading with Inquiry and Action: How Principals Improve Teaching and Learning* (2009). Militello has received funding to conduct research from the College Board, the W.K. Kellogg Foundation, Xian Normal University, and a multimillion-dollar Race to the Top grant to train school leaders in Northeast North Carolina. He is currently implementing an innovative Ed.D. degree for East Carolina University in Southeast Asia. He earned his master's and Ph.D. in educational administration from Michigan State University.